A Calypso Trilogy

Rawle A. Gibbons

Ian Randle Publishers
Kingston

Canboulay
PRODUCTIONS
Tunapuna

© 1999 Rawle A. Gibbons

First published in Jamaica 1999 by
Ian Randle Publishers
206 Old Hope Road, Box 686
Kingston 6

ISBN 976-8123-83-4 paper

A catalogue record of this book is available from the
National Library of Jamaica

First published in Trinidad and Tobago 1999 by
Canboulay Productions
#32 St. Vincent Street,
Tunapuna

ISBN 976-8056-47-9 paper

Set in Garamond
Book design by Errol Stennett

Contents

Preface

These plays attempted to popularize once again, the great music written and performed by calypsonians since the 1930s, music which our radio stations largely ignored. In their success, the plays also created a challenge for the theatre (not for the first time) to place itself in the mainstream of popular entertainment. One is grateful that these works have fulfilled their purpose and given pleasure to many over the years.

I am indebted to all who contributed to the realization of this publication. Foremost, those Calypso artists whose tradtion was it's inspiration; Claypso collectors and die-hards, the late Rocky McCollin, Teddy Pinheiro, Zeno Obi Constance, Louis Regis, Gordon Rohlehr, whose archives were always open to me. Canboulay Productions - actors, musicians, director , Louis McWilliams and producers, Michael Phillips, Margaret Walcott, Kenwyn Crichlow; typists, Yvette Barrimond and Gail McIntosh; supporting institutions, the Univeristy of the West Indies and the Festival Centre for the Creative Arts; my loving and beloved family and Him through whom everything is possible - Oludumare.

Modupe
Rawle Gibbons

Building Bridges of Song

An Introduction by Louis Regis

Calypso drama, like the calypso itself, originates in a complex of social contexts and serves a multiplicity of social roles. It is a form which can be traced to the skits first presented in the calypso tents of the 30's. The present trilogy, however, is far more ambitious and comprehensive than those early efforts. It aims at reconstructing the history of the Calypso between 1930 and 1970 while demonstrating that the Calypso is a protean art-form with immense potential for shaping into sophisticated folk-urban theatre which is simultaneously entertaining and educational.

Conventional wisdom teaches that the Calypso germinated in the cross-fertilisation of African and European literary-musical traditions, and that it blossomed in the hothouse that was 19th century Port of Spain. Earlier scholarship, fulfilling the requirements of Anthropology and Ethnomusicology, considered the Calypso in its macro aspect, that is, as a musical legacy of the enforced meeting of two cultures, and as a dynamic working out of the conflict between white superstructure and black folk. Later scholarship tended toward the biographical and the literary. Spanning both writings is the work of Professor Gordon Rohlehr, the literary scholar who pioneered the multidisciplinary approach to the study of the calypso and who authored the magisterial *Calypso and Society in Pre - Independence Trinidad*. All the while, though, other literary creatives had been employing the Calypso and the Calypsonian as metaphor and as trope.

The trilogy bridges the academic and the artistic in that it dramatizes the history of the calypso but highlights story-lines suggested by calypso fictions, narratives and commentaries. While adhering to the historical record, the trilogy incorporates and subsumes the historical account into a complex of plots and sub-plots, in which calypsonians, imaginatively reconstructed from calypsoes rather than from their biographies, are the major players. The trilogy thus restores the calypsonian to his rightful place in history by presenting the Calypso as the sum of individual and collective responses to private circumstances and public situations.

Throughout the trilogy, however, calypsoes have been re-contextualised and given new significance according to the logic of the drama. At the beginning of 'Ten to One', for example, Sparrow's 'The Slave' (first performed in 1963) serves as the background against which Dr. Eric Williams enunciates his 'Massa Day Done' address (delivered in 1961). Speech and song thus function as bi-modal discourse, as it were, for the nationalism mouthed by Williams as early as 1955. In the same play, Cristo's 'Miss Universe', a disinterested panegyric to the Miss Sweden winner of the Miss Universe title sometime in the 50s, and Sparrow's 'Jean and Dinah', a song which gloats over the distress of the Trinidad call girls abandoned by their erstwhile American servicemen lovers and clients, function as the theme music for the Miss Trinidad pageant which by 1956 had become the media event of the year. By partnering 'Miss Universe' and 'Jean and Dinah' in this way, Gibbons hints that beneath the differences of skin colour the local Snow Whites are comparable to their dusky sisters of the night immortalised in the Sparrow classic.

The point to the foregoing is that Gibbons is demonstrating that while the Calypso can be 'used' in all its traditional ways, (for example, as song of praise, censure, prophecy, lamentation, as carthasis, as self-mockery or as mockery of others, as a rite of passage for arrivantes, as dance music, as rallying call, as word-play, as source for social history, as inspiration for dance, art, literature and so on), it is also a valuable tropism which can be refashioned to serve theatre by providing inspiration for dramatic situation.

The trilogy is divided neatly into three parts each corresponding to a well-defined phase in Calypso history. 'Sing De Chorus' recreates the Golden Age of Kaisos Resurgence, that period between the Great Depression and the end of World War II when the city barrack-yard, the city and the world itself were in ferment. It was during this period that the kaisonian became something of a national cultural symbol when his championing of nationalist causes embroiled him with the colonial authorities. At the same time, the Calypso had become a craze in North America. 'Sing De Chorus' acknowledges these happenings but concludes that while the kaisonian had become a national and an international personality he still saw himself as an humble yard-dweller caught up in the trade winds of his life and times and concerned not with history but with survival.

'Ah Wanna Fall' advances the story into that post War period when the kaisonians had begun to drift out of the narrow jamet yards in pursuit of career. Metropolitan exile or early return to dust were the destiny of most of the emergent calypsonians as they wrestled tragically with a society which had not (and still has not) valued them as professional entertainers.

'Ten To One' introduces the modern age of competitiveness, exploitation and neglect. This period is dominated by the charismatic Sparrow the rebel who defied the public definition of social outcast into which the calypsonians and other folk artistes had been typecast. Sparrow's surprise Calypso King and Road March victories in 1956 followed by his 1957 boycott of the Dimanche Gras show, his public identification with Dr. Williams and his vigorous championing of the cause of folk artistes gave him a public image which supported his attempt to destroy a self-fulfilling social stereotype. Struggle he did and with some success, but one notes from 'Ten To One' that most of his energy as composer/performer went into defending his song, into justifying his actions on and offstage, into celebrating his numerous sexual conquests and into duelling first with Melody and then against Kitchener. One notes too that the demands on Sparrow as a professional entertainer removed him from centre stage just when a youthful Black Power challenged a somnolent Black presence in Parliament.

One should not lose sight of the fact that the trilogy is essentially a study in theatre. In his M. Phil thesis, 'Towards a Third Theatre: Traditional Enactments of Trinidad', Gibbons argued for a synthesis of the scribal and oral traditions inherited from three continents. His life's work at the Creative Arts Centre has been to marry the great Western traditions of European auditoriums to gayelles, the palais, and the arenas where the folk celebrate sacred and secular dramas of participation and possession. The Trilogy ventures into the yard, the tent, the streets and the several stages where the lives of calypsonians are played out; (it also glances at the platforms where politicians and other public personalities try in vain to dictate to calypsonians). Adding to these fertile sources of drama, the trilogy accesses the Calypso itself as a major source of character and conflict.

The trilogy offers itself as an experience in 20th century theatre styles. It harmonizes the kinesis of the folk experience with the avant garde experiments of the folk-oriented playwrights, and thus maximises the possibilities for seamless fit of multiple plots, for fluid transformations in time, place and action, for innovative use of set, props, costume, lighting and the like, for the incorporation of music, dance and choric movement, and for the involvement of the audience.

Overwhelmingly enthusiastic response on the part of the public testifies that the productions were a welcome feast in a land long hungering for both kaiso and good theatre. Tony Hall's 'Jean and Dinah' (1994), Zeno Obi Constance's 'De Roaring Seventies' (1994) and Rhoma Spencer's 'Bassman' (1997) took their cue and indications are that young playwrights, following Gibbons' lead, are beginning to seek inspiration in the theatre and song of the folk.

Sing De Chorus

(Classic Calypsoes of the 1930s - 1940s)

Characters

TOWN RAT

MADAME DOROTHY KHAN

BATTLER

SAGA

RADIO / BUTLER

WINSTON (CRUSADER)

LOUISE /LADY IERE

CORPORAL SANTAPEE

INSPECTOR-GENERAL OF POLICE

GRAND:: OLD LADY / JANET

CIPRIANI / PA GOMES

TIMER

ATILLA

EXECUTOR

MATILDA

The play was first produced by Canboulay Productions in January 1991. The production was directed by Louis McWilliams with the following cast:

TOWN RAT- David Scobie
MADAME DOROTHY KHAN- Sharon Devenish
BATTLER- Clem Haynes
SAGA- Phillip Murray
RADIO / BUTLER- Brian Honore
WINSTON (CRUSADER)- Kurtis Gross
LOUISE /LADY IERE- Ucill Cambridge
CORPORAL SANTAPEE- Christopher Shepperd
INSPECTOR-GENERAL OF POLICE- Errol Jones
GRAND OLD LADY / JANET- Rhoda Reddock
CIPRIANI / PA GOMES- Michael Gonzales
TIMER/ Atilla- Leon Roach
EXECUTOR- Willard Phillip
MATILDA- Denise Dickson / Kandisann Harry

Musicians

MUSICAL DIRECTOR /CUATRO- Desmond Waithe
GUITARS- Michael Gonzales / Willard Phillip
FLUTE- Cuthbert Fletcher
SAXOPHONE- Percy Oblington
BASS- Alisford Phillips

Calypsoes

SING DE CHORUS-CAST
MADAME KHAN-Caresser
WOMAN CALLED DOROTHY-Executor

SONGS OF LONG AGO-Invader
SANS HUMANITE- Gibbons
A MOTHER'S LOVE-Destroyer
SAGA FELLARS IN TOWN-Lady Iere
COLDNESS OF THE WATER-Growler
TREASURY SCANDAL-Atilla
COUNTRY CLUB SCANDAL-Growling Tiger / Brian Honore /
Rawle Gibbons
REIGN TOO LONG -Executor
TRIBUTE TO EXECUTOR- Lord Iere
LEAVE ME ALONE DOROTHY- Destroyer
LOS IROS-Growling Tiger
ST. PETER'S DAY-Lord Beginner
LOVE ME OR LEAVE ME-Lady Iere
UGLY WOMAN- Roaring Lion
TROUBLE AND MISERY-Lord Beginner
GRAF ZEPPELIN-Atilla
DEW AND RAIN-the Growler
HISTORY OF CARNIVAL-Atilla
MATILDA-King Radio
PARAMARIBO-Caresser
THE GOLD IN AFRICA-Growling Tiger
WORKERS' PLEA-Growling Tiger
TRY A SCREW-Growling Tiger
BLACK MARKET-Lord Beginner
MONEY IS KING-Growling Tiger
FOUR CENTS A DAY-Atilla
MAN SANTAPEE-Atilla
IN MY OWN NATIVE LAND-Growling Tiger
SEDITION LAW-King Radio
LOUISE-Lord Beginner
ADOLF HITLER-Destroyer
RUM AND COCA-COLA- Invader
LET THE WHITE PEOPLE FIGHT-Growling Tiger
WHICH IS THE BEST-King Radio/Roaring Lion

Act 1 (1934)

*A Port of Spain tenement yard in the early 1930's. The yard,
La Cou Kaiso, is set for its famous calypso tent.*

*Prologue:the band runs through a medley of the evening's
calypsoes, ending with the theme song: 'Sing De Chorus' led
by the Shantwelle 'Saga':*

Chorus: Sing de Chorus O!
              Heroes of war, La Cou Kaiso

Saga: Atilla, Radio, Executor
              Back in town to deal with the censor

Battler: If you want to know about calypso
              Then you have to check out King Radio

Saga: Lord Invader and Growling Tiger
              Roaring Lion and the Pretender

Winston: Warn them other tent in Port of Spain
              That we are the La Cou hurricane

Dorothy: If them other tent step outa line
              We go make them do the dollar wine

Timer: In centuries to come I'll have them know
              That people will still sing calypso.

              *(Lines should be extemporised. Cast disperse
              to positions for Scene 1)*

Scene I

Town Rat: *(Enters from street)* Radio! Radio, oye!

Dorothy: *(Tumbles Battler out of her room)*
You take me for a damn fool? Take that. And this!

Town Rat: Morning, Madame Khan.

Battler: O God, Dorothy, I beg you take it easy. Is the
truth.

Dorothy: And I is Madame Jackass! You ain't find you
brave to try that with a woman like me, eh Battler?

Battler: People lying on me.

Dorothy: Look at me, Battler, and look at you. You ain't
find you brave?

Battler   Dors, you is more woman than any man could
want.

Dorothy: Answer me! You ain't find you brave and bold and
brass-face to take chances with a woman like
Dorothy Khan?

Battler: Yes, Dorothy, I brave....

Dorothy: Since you so brave, take this! And that! And as for
you, morning my backside! *(Exits to her room)*

Town Rat: Pleasant day to you too, ma'am.

Saga: (MADAME KHAN)
Chorus:I say to hold your hand, Madame Khan
I mean to hold your hand, Madame Khan
I say hold your hand, Madame Khan
You will hear the same from woman and man

When talking about a woman bad like crab
I mean your heart and soul and all she will grab
Cut out your pocket and leave you to groan
Then beat you with big stick, bottle and stone

Well I never see another human like that
She boast how she big, she strong, and she fat
The female Canera a heavyweight
Breaking down the scale at two ninety-eight

Battler: *(Joins in song after a stanza or two)*
Well I never see a woman with a right hand so
One cuff from she nail me to a door
You could believe,O loss I really thought I was dead
When a nail in the door went right through my head

Town Rat: *(At the end of song)* I now see why they call you
Battler. You could really fight.

Radio: Hush all you tail out there! A man trying to sleep!

Town Rat: Radio! Wake up, boy! I have one for you.

Radio: Dorothy break Battler tail again. I sing that already.

Town Rat: I talking 'bout high-class scandal, boy, not no
barrack-yard business. White people bacchanal!
Do fast, else is down by Railroad Millionaires tent
I gone.

Radio: Wait, wait, nuh. Move over woman, this is serious business.

Saga: So Town Rat, what town say is really true?

Town Rat: What town say?

Saga: You know, about them white people, it really happen?

Town Rat: Don't try that with me, Saga. How much you paying? This one hot boy.

Saga: Pay? And I getting topic right in me doormouth?
I will stick to my barrack-yard z'affaire, eh Battler?
(Begins to compose song: WOMAN CALLED DOROTHY*)*
I was weak and broken down
All my nerves shattered and worn
Who caused that cruelty to me
None other but a woman called Dorothy

Radio: *(Emerging)* What is the wire?

Town Rat: Usual arrangement. Twenty percent of yours is mine.

Radio: Talk, nuh. I don't even know if a kaiso could come out of your ol' talk yet.

Town Rat: This one from the horse's mouth, boy. You make kaiso with less. Besides, you know Town Rat could smell a rumour a mile off.

Radio: So what you have?

Town Rat: *(Whispers to him)*

Radio: The Inspector-General of Police? You sure?

Town Rat: The husband heself tell somebody who know
                somebody who know my contact who in turn tell
                me. The man want a kaiso bad, and he ain't care
                who sing it.

Radio: Alright. Who this husband is?

Town Rat: *(Whispers)*

Radio: *(Laughs)* I like it.

Town Rat: Is good material or not?

Radio: I hearing the song already.

Town Rat: Thirty percent?

Radio: Haul you...! You want to make the kaiso and sing it
                yourself?

Town Rat: Just joking.

Radio: Go and joke down by the printery. Tell Baje I want
                a hundred flyers for the show tonight.

Town Rat: What he must put on them?

Radio: What else? Radio singing the latest social bacchanal
                The Country Club Scandal!

Saga: I have it!

Town Rat: *(Exits to street)*

Radio: *(Exits to room)*

Saga: *(Teases Battler,* WOMAN CALLED DOROTHY)
Chorus:
I was weak and broken down
All my nerves shattered and torn
Who caused that cruelty to me
No other but a woman called Dorothy

Now Dorothy a nice high brown
Weighing two-hundred and sixty pound
And I (Battler) is a feather weight
She make me tremble like an earthquake

Timer: *An old calypsonian comes out of his room to join Saga
and Battler in the song.*
She told me (darling) you must stay with me
Brutalize me and you can even beat me
Do what you like you could tear up me clothes
Cause you know I'm a woman that love your blows

Winston: *(Enters from the street)*
Excuse me, sirs, I looking for Mr. Radio
the calypsonian.

Saga: Mr. Radio?

Battler: Where he from, boy?

Winston:: Siparia. This is La Cou Kaiso where Mr. Radio
does run the calypso tent?

Timer: What you want with Radio, son?

Winston: I come to sing in he tent.

Timer: Hmm!

Battler: Just so?

Saga: Sing what? Port of Spain people don't want to
               hear 'Ba Ba Black Sheep' and 'Sleep Petite Popo'
               you know. This is La Cou Kaiso, where only the
               masters does meet.

Battler: Last time I sing down Siparee.... you recognise who
               talking to you?

Winston: I ain't think so.

Saga: The Mighty Battler, boy!

Winston: Battler?

Battler: What they know down in Siparee? Last time I sing
               down there, people did think the roadmarch was
               still: 'Rah te rah te ray, te ray te ray.
               Cola dead and gone.
               Rah te rah te ray, te ray te ray.
               Cola dead and gone'
               (SONGS OF LONG AGO)
               Some people argue the songs of long ago}
               Used to be better calypso   } Repeat
               They must be mad
               Can you remember wai, yai, yai, madam o, latey la
               And then they sang

               Chorus:
               Ra te ra te ray, te ray te ray
               Cola dead and gone
               Ah say de leggo was
               Ra te ra te ray, te ray te ray
               Cola dead and gone

I'm sure most of you all can remember
Henry Forbes, Pastille and Malborough
And King Fanto from San Fernando
Those were the songsters of long ago
They used to sing 'married man in the slaughtery,
Sweet man eating talcari
You run, you run, you run and why you run'
And then they sang

Chorus

Now I remind you of a song they used to sing
long time
But they did not use to sing it in rhyme
They never used to rhyme in the correct way
 Like the modern songsters today
They used to sing: 'Tina, where you went
I went to tie me clothes in the bamboo'
And then

Chorus

And today we put rhythm in the calypso
Have you heard 'Take me down to Los Iros
And don't ley me mama know'
And 'Thousand, ten thousand to bar me one'
Thousand, ten thousand to bar me one
And long time was

Chorus

Timer: That is kaiso, no use getting vex. Plenty licks and a
empty belly. The only fat you will get outa kaiso is
fatigue. Go and pick up a trade.

Winston: I win the competition in Siparia. They tell me
though I young, I could make in the city.

Saga: Win from who? Lord Cassava and the Mighty
            Banana? You better catch the midday.

Timer: What sort of kaiso you does sing?

Winston: How you mean?

Timer: Well, it could be lavway...

Battler: Or topical...

Saga: Double or single tone...

Battler: In the major or minor, key that is...

Timer: And most of all what is your genealogy?

Winston: Geneawho? All I come to do is sing kaiso.

Radio: *(Emerging)* I have it! Fellas, take a taste!
            (Opening lines of COUNTRY CLUB SCANDAL)
            Scandal big bacchanal   }
            That take place at the Country Club carnival }repeat
            The sweetman and he lady went to spend the day
            But the husband find out the lacouray
            He meet the man

Battler: Man, give we the rest, Radio.

Radio: Tonight, tonight.

Winston: Mr. Radio.

Radio: Mr. Radio? Who you is, boy?

Saga: Lord Zaboca, Calypso King of Siparee.

Winston: I does sing calypso and hoping you will give me a chance to sing in your tent.

Radio: First thing, I is Radio, plain Radio or King Radio, but no 'Mr.' Next thing people will think I decent! You say you does sing kaiso?

Winston: I win the Chenette Corner Grand Finals in Siparia.

Radio: Chord, fellas.

(Band Introduces 'SANS HUMANITE')
Chorus: It is not now in my mind}
To make rebellion in this Iere Land   } repeat
But is the terrible condition
Of this rising generation
In this Iere Land
Is the terrible condition
Of this rising generation
Sans Humanite.

Radio: Young man you now step outa short pants
You jump in the ring bawling 'gimme a chance'
You ain't even drop your milk teeth
You find your way from Siparee to Charlotte Street.
But do you know the genealogy
Of this great art, I mean, its ancestry
You can't just come off the tram
And call yourself calypsonian
Sans Humanite.

Winston: I am King Winston from Siparee
All over the South nobody beat me
True, I young in the kaiso art
But my grandfather say for me there's a part
So I follow the star of my destiny

It take me from the country to the city
I ain't turning back without the fortunes of victory
Sans Humanite.

Radio: You can't step in the Hall of Fame
'Til you pay tribute to the greatest names
Have you ever heard of the slave Gros Jean
Whose voice was so sweet it calmed Begorrat?
Cedric Le Blanc, the great white shantwelle
And women like Bodicea and Petit Belle
Do you even know
Who sang the first English kaiso?
Sans Humanite.

Winston: I am not versed in this art, I know
That's why I come to La Cou Kaiso
If you want to pick up the rules
Experience, they say, is the greatest school
So I set my heart on fame to find
Leaving my friends, grandparents behind
I know I could sing
Look I throw my hat down in the ring
Sans Humanite.

Radio: Young man, it is clear you are ambitious
But voice alone can't make you come first
Duke of Malborough, Senior Inventor
Julian White Rose and Executor
These are the names that will ever endure
Their voice was one with the oppressed and poor
Or to the art bring new energy
Like Roaring Lion and Yours Truly.

Santapee: *(Enters from street)*   Radio, this flyer is yours?

Radio: Corporal Santapee, good day to you.
I hope like all bad news you ain't staying around.

Santapee: I ask whether this flyer is or is not belonging to you? It say you intend to sing a calypso tonight called the 'Country Club Scandal'. Is that so?

Radio: God willing.

Santapee: Well, the law ain't willing. I want to inform you that any such song will be deem libelous, the maximum penalty for which offence is a fine of $500.00 and six months at her Majesty's pleasure.

Radio: Man, you don't even know what the song will say. How you could say is libel?

Santapee: Is a calypso, not so? And what it talking 'bout ain't nobody business but the people concern. You is not to sing it.

Timer: Hold on, Corporal. What law say Radio can't sing this song he make that nobody even hear yet?

Santapee: You want me show you the law? This. *(Shows his truncheon)* The whole of Port of Spain know Corporal Santapee law, not so?

Timer: That sound like a threat, boy.

Santapee: What you is? A barrack-yard magistrate? You want me take you down by the station old as you is, and give you a good lesson in the law?

Dorothy: What going on here? *(Opening her door)* Battler, what happen?

Battler: Radio.....

Santapee: I just pull he plug.

Dorothy: Sanatpee, wherever you is, is trouble for black people.

Santapee: Black people does bring trouble on theyself. They born in trouble and is so they go dead. My work is just to make sure they don't spread their disease among decent folk.

Dorothy: And you is nothing more than their dog. *(Dog calls)* 'Come, Rover'. 'Sik 'im, Rover'. Don't play no police for me, you know. I know you as a chigger-foot boy up and down in the market begging for food. Your mother must be turning in she grave.

Santapee: She good there. If she was alive I would run she off the streets for the whore she was.

Dorothy: Boy, what you say about your mother?
God forgive you.

Santapee: You know so much and you ain't know that? So don't feel I fraid to do the same for every jagabat and every calypsonian in this yard. Radio, remember. *(Exits)*

Timer: A man who cuss he mother is the scourge of the earth.

Dorothy: (A MOTHER'S LOVE
Other women enter yard with song.)
A mother's love we cannot forget   }
Wrong things we do we bound to regret } repeat
You can have money in a quantity
And have a lot of friends in society

You can have diamonds, rubies and pearls
A mother's love is the master key of this world

Children your mother you must consider
Try and be moderate in your behaviour
You must be loving and generous
And your days will be prosperous
Don't give her any back chat or insolence
For you would be punished by the Omnipotent
A mother's love was blessed from creation
You could never find a great and stronger affection

Blessed be the child that love its mother
Happy shall be its days forever
It shall be blessed with prosperity
And showers of love from the Almighty
But if you are rude believe it or not
An ungrateful child it reaps a short crop
And the ending of his day will be so bitter
That it might die without a spoonful of cold water

Winston: He could really stop you from singing, Radio?

Radio: *(Shrugs)* Perils of kaiso life, boy.

Timer: In kaiso if people don't like what you singing you can't eat; when people want your song is police bootoo on your back. Kaiso not even a dog's life.

Louise: *(One of the women now busy about the yard)*
You still in it.

Timer: It in me, in my blood. Kaiso done squeeze me dry. But for a young man, best you plant garden.

Radio: You could sing tonight. But don't expect no money. I ain't hiring you, not even as a helper. I just giving you a chance.

Winston: You ain't go be sorry, sir.

Radio: Not me. Is you to breaks if the people don't like what you singing. And let me warn you, no slackness, no smut. I have my crookstick! Fellas, I feel this situation call for help from higher up.

Timer: Is only one man will stand by calypsonians at a time like this.

Saga: We all know who that is, so what we waiting on?

Battler: 'Young girl, who you voting for?'

Chorus: Cipriani

Radio: We don't want Santapee make bassa-bassa here.

Chorus: Cipriani

Timer: One man who could put a stop to this whole affair.

Chorus: Cipriani   *(They exit to the street singing)*

Louise: Country, you eager to sing, but you can't sing in La Cou Kaiso looking so. You walk with your jacket?

Winston: My name is Winston. No, I ain't walk with no jacket. You have one to lend me?

Louise: But you well boldface, Mr. Winston. You now reach and you like these town fellas already -want to live off a woman.

Winston: Is only the jacket I asking for, Miss..............?

Louise: Hear him, nuh! And he have words to boot. You learning well fast.

Winston: I intend to reach the top. Bet you next season I up there with the best.

Louise: It take more than boasting to make it in kaiso, you ain't even prove yourself yet. Tonight will tell.

Winston: I willing to prove myself anytime, Miss.....?

Louise: Louise, that is my name, right?

Winston: Louise, like breeze through the leaves.....

Louise: You sure you not from some part of town?

Winston: No, but I feel at home already.

Louise: That is because you just as watless and dangerous as these Port of Spain men. You is definitely a man to stay far from.

Winston: Just so? What I do?

Louise: (SAGA FELLAS IN TOWN)
Not me to confuse me brains   }
With the saga fellars in Port-Of-Spain } repeat
That kind of love only goodness knows
Licks like fire, no food, no clothes

All day long they sit and lahay
I must work, they must get the pay
That's why

Chorus:
I wouldn't be so fast to tell you look for work
They say macomere you making joke
You bet your life, they rather live in jail
And every weekend receive the cat o nine tail

Now hear the dangerous plan
They want a million rings on they hand
A gold chain expose on they chest
And their affection for you is blest
Every Monday is a suit length
And all the time I losing me strength
All day long they sit and lahay
I must work they must get the pay
That's why

Chorus

For this love girl prepare yuh back
They have a kind of brutal attack
Make a rounds and see what you get
I and the boys want to have a fete
For if you fail is so much high fall
Like Putty Lewis be on the ball
The only recompense for me
Is P.H. or the cemetery

*(Transition song during which set is adjusted
for "La Cou Kaiso" tent Cipriani enters audience)*

Saga: *(As M.C.)* Come, come, a round of applause for
the leading lady calypsonian in Trinidad and

Tobago, ladies and gentlemen, Lady Iere! At La
Cou Kaiso tent we give you only the best. *(Ad lib
M.C. style)*.   The next singer is new to Port of
Spain. He beat all comers hands down in
Siparia and battle his way to the Big Yard. Fair is
fair, and tonight ladies and gentleman, you are the
judge as to whether this young man have a future in
the calypso world. I give you, the Siparia Kid!

Winston: *(Entering)* Good evening, ladies and gentlemen, I
just want to say thanks to King Radio for giving me
this chance. Since I reach in Port of Spain, people
only asking how come I leave the South. Well, let
me give you the story.

(COLDNESS OF THE WATER)
It seem as though mi wife going mad   }
Because I left the South she talk me bad   } repeat

Chorus:
The coldness of the water
Nearly kill (Siparia) dead

She said to me huzy you must be bold
Because the dipping in the river bound to free you soul
If that is the road to find the Lord
Not me she wouldn't send me in the P.H. ward

To bless me soul I was more than glad
But when they dip me in the river I felt so bad
Water in me nose, all inside me mouth
To hear the congregation how they start to shout

They took me up to the mourning ground
And all I saw was lighted candles all around

Candles start to roll back to number three
They said I'm on the way to Galilee

Chorus

The teacher tell me when I reach to Galilee
All my sins will be washed away entirely
But I got too much tied and burden down
Because I never reach no further than the mourning
ground

Louise: *(At end of song)* Siparia! look my key! *(Throws key for
him Santapee and Inspector-General enter tent.)*

Saga: Off to a good start, lad. Don't forget to give back
the jacket you borrow. I see we are having a visit
from our friends of the law. We are honoured.
Gentlemen, enjoy the show. Our next singer is a
staunch defender of Calypso, a fearless fighter for
the liberties of the people's art and indeed a great
calypsonian himself. He has given us classics like
'The Graf Zeppelin', 'Guardian Beauty Contest' and
'Reply to the Daily Mail'. Ladies and gentlemen,
none other than Atilla the Hun!

Atilla: (TREASURY SCANDAL)
I wonder if it's boboll   }
What they doing with taxpayer's money at all} repeat
All around the town you can hear the talk
Two hundred thousand dollars can' take a walk
People saying is conspiracy
I mean the scandal in the Treasury

It was about just eight months past
That the whole of Trinidad stood aghast
When the Government made a declaration

That created a great sensation
In the books of the Treasury something went wrong
Two hundred thousand dollars could not be found
And every clerk say it ain't they fault
So it must be a spirit open the vault.

Well now the entire population
Have demanded an explanation
For when to balance his books the poor clerk fail
They took him to court and sent him to jail
Some say in baccara their money loss
Others declare that they buy racehorse
That someone stole it we can't deny
For money ain't got wings and it cannot fly

Well I would not have made this song at all
But I ain't get nothing in the boboll
While I poor Atilla seeing hell
They carry way cash and they doing well
For two hundred thousand take it from me
I would make five years quite happily
And when I come from jail what the deuce I care
I'd be living the life of a millionaire

Saga: *(Introduces Radio)* A talk going around, ladies and
gents, about what happen between a lady and her
gentlemen last night in a certain place. Everybody
want to know, but nobody talking. Well, this next
singer was on the scene and he's here to tell us about
it. The singer you have been waiting for. King Radio
and his 'Country Club Scandal.'

Santapee: Radio! You done get warn!

Atilla: Ladies and gentlemen, we seem to have a problem
here. You come to hear this kaiso, but the police say

Radio must not sing it. You see, this time the
bacchanal is not in the barrack yard, it is in the
high-brow Country Club and it involves those who
should be exemplars in this society. So the police
here to make sure you ain't hear that song. They
come to protect, once
again the interest of the privileged. But I don't
intend to make a political platform of this tent. I
ain't ready for the Legislative Council yet. You pay
your money to hear kaiso and is for you, the people,
the Calypsonian does sing. You want to hear
'Country Club Scandal', yes or no?.

Audience: (RESPONSE.)

Atilla: Vox Populi, vox Dei! Radio, sing your kaiso, boy!

Santapee: Let me see if Vox Populi making the jail with you!

Radio: Atilla, the man say he go lock me up.

Cipriani: *(Rising from audience)* Radio, sing your song. There is
no law preventing any citizen of this colony, thank
God, from singing a song that is not libelous. You
call any names?

Radio: I smarter than that, Captain.

Cipriani: Then they will have to lock me up too. Put a chair
on that stage for me. Sing your song, young man,
and let the police do their damndest! *(Sits on stage)*

Inspector: Let it go, Corporal. Let the politicians have their
day. There's more than one way to skin a cat. Stay
here and take note of every word he says. *(Exits)*

Radio: (COUNTRY CLUB SCANDAL)
Scandal, big bachannal
That take place at the Country Club, carnival } repeat
The sweetman and the lady went to spend the day
But the husband find out the lacouray
He meet he wife naked as she born
And the sweetman without he uniform

Chorus:
Naked you come, naked you go
The husband tell she in kaiso
Naked you come, naked you go
But the sweetman knock him down with a poe
Naked you come, naked you go (twice)

The President of the tennis court
Intervened was to stop the wrath
They grab onto he jacket
And they beat him with a tennis racket
The husband call the sweetman a fool
The sweetman throw him in the swimming pool
And while the white people having fun
I ketch the Corporal thiefing the rum

Naked you come, naked you go
No woman can't do that to Radio
Naked you come, naked you go
I would have pack she back to Palo Seco

The husband now getting wild
But the wife only watching him with a smile
She grinning like a Chesire cat
He slap she with an alpagat
Darling I don't believe what I see
I mean to say, you never do that to me

She turn and tell she husband with scorn
My boy blue have a better horn

Naked you come , naked you go
What the sweetman name all you want to know
Naked you come , naked you go
All you want Santapee to lock up Radio
Naked you come, naked you go (Sing it out boys)
This is the King Radio

Radio: *(Picongs Santapee until he leaves)*
Let me show you how life ain't fair
For example, what happen tonight here
The boss say, 'Now, Corporal Lackey,
Write every word down, that's your duty'
He leave with out a backward glance
And throw the man in a monkey pants
'Cause he can't tell
But the Corporal don't know how to spell
Sans Humanite

Atilla: *(Joining Radio on stage)*
How absurd in this colony
Where it was born Calypso is not yet free
If Kaiso is indecent then I must insist
So is Shakespeare's 'Venus and Adonis'
Police spies always snooping around
Taking shorthand notes of my song
In centuries to come, I'd have them know
People will still sing calypso
Sans Humanite.

Santapee: Don't worry. Every boar-hog have he Saturday.
(Exits)

Saga: To you we bid good riddance
So now we give the entertainment a chance

Now let me invite those of you who know
To come on stage and sing in extempo
(Sponsor's name) is our kind sponsor
So tonight we sing in their honour
The prize as you see
In this box remains a mystery
Sans Humanite.

(Opens invitation to audience to sing on stage).

Executor: *(Enters from audience)*
I was just passing outside this hall
When I heard the sound of your bugle call
Summoning all heroes from near and far
To rise in full voice and enter the war
So I must live up to my name
All pretenders kneel before me in shame
I am Executor, til forever
The Master mi minor, Sans Humanite.
(Sings on topic)

(REIGN TOO LONG)

Chorus:
They say I reign too long
Forgetting that my constitution is strong
Instead of glorifying my long years reign
They making plot to bring down me name

When every hair on Queen Victoria's head
Was turning white England never said
She is too old to sit on the throne
They allow her to remain and control her own

Chorus

When Jack Hobbs was fifty-three
He was still batting quite splendidly
And so you'll find every word in me
Is a boundary right round this colony

Chorus

We all recommend a precious wine
That is kept in the cellar for a length of time
Connoisseurs declare it will make you bold
Healthy, vigorous and cold

Saga: Ladies and gentlemen, we will pass the bouquet on
behalf of the Lord Executor, this genius who lives
and will die for the art. No praise, none, ladies and
gentlemen, is equal to the sacrifice, the sheer genius
of this man, calypso's greatest hero. Let us merely
be thankful that he has given his life, his remarkable
talents to this art we call calypso.

(TRIBUTE TO EXECUTOR)
Calypsonians will come, calypsonians have gone}
But his name forever lives on} repeat
Turn back the pages of history
And I'm sure you'll agree with me
Executor was a warrior
Executor was a terror
True boss in the ray minor

Hear what he sang
Malaria, epidemic in the land   }
City Council give the command } repeat
It was given to the rich and poor
Put your rubbish in front yuh door
Belmont disgrace

And Woodbrook second place
Sans Humanite

Well in the year 1925
Gorrie took Olga's corrupted life
Eleven o'clock we heard the shocking news
The whole town was confused
That very night, they held a competition
To prove who was champion calypsonian
Executor took the occasion
He was a sensation
As the leading calypsonian
Hear what he sang

Was it madness or jealousy   }
That caused the St. James tragedy } repeat
Armed with a dagger, a razor, a knife
Gorrie took Olga's corrupted life
For his cruelty, he must pay the penalty
Sans Humanite

1934 I'm sure
No one here cannot ignore
We had quite a few tragedies
In January and February
Around 7:30 one night
A man blow off his head with a dynamite
And at nine the whole tent applaud
He sang the tragedies of 1934

Hear me, the new year opens as far as I see}
With lots of crimes and catastrophe   } repeat
A motor car crash
A little boy get mash
A woman loss her life in a razor slash
The dynamite roar

The tragedies of 1934
Sans Humanite.

(During song, Executor receives prize / bouquet. Exits to sound of bass alone. Inspector-general, Corporal Santapee and "Grand old lady of St. Vincent Street" - the Port of Spain Gazette - enter in a dame lorraine dance)

Grand: We hereby announce the Theatres and Dance Halls Ordinance, this year of our Lord, nineteen hundred and thirty-four!

Inspector: Why do you look so surprised?
It's just tyranny once more in disguise
Bringing you the latest news
Censorship on calypso is now approved

Chorus:
Now's the time for the police to dance
Theatres and Dance Halls Ordinance
Watch your tongue, we ain't giving no chance
Theatres and Dance Halls Ordinance

Inspector: Every word I must see
Before you sing it, that is my authority
Keep it clean, if you can
That damn 'Country Club Scandal' I hereby ban!

Inspector: I go be sole authority
You bound to pay for what you do to me
Right in the Council I moving me motion
Tell Cipriani, it's Executive action!

Inspector: Lose the battle but win the war
I bounce back boys, much stronger than before

Is death to calypso this time for sure
You wanted law? Well, take de law! *(They exit)*

Scene II

Battler: *(Grand charging in front of Madame Khan's door)*

(LEAVE ME ALONE DOROTHY)
Chorus:
Leave me alone Dorothy
You better leave me alone Dorothy
Because your intention
Is to kill me with indigestion

It was a kind of sauce from a bottle
That had me brain stumble
I believe that its composition
Start to change my complexion

Chorus

My complaint was a serious matter
Day by day my hair getting shorter
Necromancy had me red-handed
In my young days getting bald-pated

Chorus

Saga: You playing bobolee for Jouvert? Wait till she come out.

Battler: I looking chupid? She ain't home. But sometimes I does really wonder if is something in my food.

Timer: You does still wonder?

Saga: Don't mind Timer. He living alone all these years, what he know 'bout woman? Is not the food, is the licks, the constant licks you getting that affecting your head.

Battler: You really think so, Saga?

Timer: What ain't meet you don't pass you, nuh. If my head wasn't sharp, all now I end up like you or Saga.

Saga: What you mean by that now? I control my woman as everybody know.

Battler: Some woman nearly catch you, Timer boy?

Timer: (LOS IROS)
She's a girl in society
She never drink rum neither whiskey
I gave her a crown of Crown Lion piece
And I took her down on Los Iros beach

Chorus:
Take me , take me
I am feeling lonely
Take me down to Los Iros
But don't let me mother know

I told her I were home at my family
And they giving me dinner, breakfast and tea
And if I promise you to marry to me
I'll be putting myself into misery

She said to me
Take me, take me, take me, take me, take me
Darling only please won't you take me

Take me down to Los Iros
But don't let the old queen know.

Saga: You had your day. Well, I still having mine.

(ST. PETER'S DAY)
Chorus:
I can remember St. Peter's Day
I followed the crowd down to Teteron bay
The water in the bay was as cold as ice
All I heard then was daddy you nice

My position was financial
I said today will be bachannal
For the short and the tall one fell on her knee
Don't ask how I pelt me foot in the sea

Dorothy had on a bathing suit
You can imagine how she was looking cute
I did not mind the water was cold
For I cuff them down like a young creole

Under the water was looking dark
I felt something held me just like a shark
But when I looked it was Caroline
She said drink your rum and let me get mine

Winston: (*Enters from Louise's room*)

Timer: Aye, Wonderboy, you sleep late.

Saga: Watch how he glowing! Like you reach heaven last night.

Battler: Lodging is one thing but you have to watch what you eating.

Louise: Battler, don't think I ain't hearing you. Why you
             don't wash your mouth from people business? It
             smelling.

Battler: Just so? I ain't say nothing to the woman.

Timer: Your luck.

Saga: What happen, Lou? You itchy this morning. Last
             night wasn't enough?

Louise: *(Entering)* Whatever last night was, Saga, was ten
             times more than you could dream to give or get!

Saga: I have a calypso to make 'bout you, you know.

Louise: Go ahead. You want me to help you remember
             some of the questions you put and when?

Timer: Hmm!

Winston: Cool down, Lou.

Louise: Don't get into this.

Saga: Yeah, keep out. I like Lou hot. Girl, I tell you
             already, I have something stash away for the two of
             we. Just say the word.

Louise: Keep it for your woman. I pay my own rent, thank
             you. *(To Winston)*
             You see how town men do women? I lay my cards
             straight. I ain't standing no sweetman pressure.

Winston: Girl, all I come in town to do is to sing kaiso.

Louise: As if singing is all it have to kaiso.

(LOVE ME OR LEAVE ME)
The men in the town
I say they blooming eyes is too long } repeat
Well you does cook they food
You does wash they clothes
When you do a wrong thing
They does give you blows
But that wouldn't do
So let me tell them what is me view

Chorus:
They've got to love me or leave me
Or live with Miss Dorothy
The time is too hard
For me to keep a man that is bad

From morning to night
You working with them you treating them right
They leave you alone
With Irene and Jane they gone out to roam
This time you pounding the table down
Cleaning ground for mouse to run on
And as you talk hard
A stick in you back, you out in the yard

Chorus

And when they come home
Butter in they mouth
This is the old talk
Darling sugar plum, choonks, I went for a walk
You like a fool you feeling so glad
Hugging and kissing as if you mad
And when you hear the wire
Is Thelma, Irene or Wilhemina

Chorus

> Young girls have more care
> And warn your boys that they must prepare
> To lose one caress
> You lose a part of your happiness
> You washing, you keeping your mister clean
> I don't see why a woman should intervene
> This Irene, Thelma and Jane
> Thief yuh man they upset yuh brain

Winston: Don't worry. Ain't you see last night how the people love me? Just now I on my feet with enough for the two of us. *(Kiss lightly. She exits to room)*

Saga: Which picture you learn that from?

Winston: Radio sleeping?

Timer: He gone to get permission from the police to sing a new kaiso. With this law is every word they have to pass before you could open your mouth.

Battler: As if it wasn't hard enough already. Sometimes you know I does really feel like mashing up Santapee and the whole Police Force. When I get ignorant, I 's a real beast, you know.

Timer: We know, Battler, we know.

Saga: We could see.

Battler: Is only this set a patience that the Lord give me.

Matilda: *(Crosses from room)* See you later, Sugar.

Saga: How much later? And what in that bag?

Matilda: O God, Saga, and I ask you if I could go to the seamstress today and you say okay? Well, this is the new material.

Saga: Don't take long. I nearly hungry.

Matilda: Food done cook, darling.

Saga: So what you want me to do? Serve meself? Just now you go tell me I have to wash the plate after I done eat. Look woman, go fast and come back before I change me mind.

Matilda: Oh thank you, peckins. Back in minutes.
(Blows him a kiss, exiting hastily)

Saga: You see how to treat oman? I don't know how big men does have 'oman beating them up and telling them what and what not to do. All you don't be shame?

Timer: What ain't meet you ain't pass you.

Saga: Say what you want, my philosophy plain and simple. Look at Matilda. True, she does dress nice and thing but she just ain't much to look at. And I like it so. Country, you take my advice:

(UGLY WOMAN)
If you want to be happy living a King's life}
Never make a pretty woman your wife }repeat
All you've got to do is just what I say
Then you will be jolly, merry and gay
From a logical point of view
Always love a woman uglier than you.

A pretty woman makes her husband look small
I mean and very often cause his downfall
As soon as she marries then and there she'll start
Doing little things that will ache his heart
And when you think she belongs to you
She's calling somebody else dou dou too
Therefore from a logical point of view
Always love a woman uglier than you

Look if you make an ugly woman your wife
You can be sure you'll be happy in all your life
For she would never do things in a funny way
To allow the neighbours to have anything to say
And she wouldn't disregard you at all
By exhibiting herself to Peter and Paul
So from a logical point of view
Always love a woman uglier than you

An ugly woman gives you your meals on time
And she will always try to satisfy your mind
At night when you lay upon your cosy bed
She will coax, caress you and scratch your head
Like a bird she'll call you nice names like Silver beak
Toy choonks, toy toy and sikia matee
Therefore from a logical point of view
Always love a woman uglier than you

Battler: It have another side to that from what I hear.
Listen, Siparia:
(TROUBLE AND MISERY)
There's an argument going around the world
All about the pretty and ugly girl} Repeat
They say the pretty girl would make you shame
Because she have the looks so she can't be blame
But if you want trouble and misery
Give an ugly woman matrimony

With an ugly woman you wouldn't have a friend
And your happy days bound to meet an end
If you are invited to a dance
You will only be taking a sporting chance
While happy couples are dancing round
She will be the laughing stock and the clown
So if you want trouble and misery
Give an ugly woman matrimony

A pretty girl she will be the pride of your heart
She wouldn't have to make up for her to look smart
Pretty dresses will fill her heart with joy
And she bound to call you papa-toi-loy
Give her what she needs and then she wouldn't frown
And I'm sure that she wouldn't let you down
But if you want trouble and misery
Give an ugly woman matrimony

If you looking for a girl friend to make you glad
Don't take an ugly woman to make you sad
For at night when you going to sleep you will frown
When you watch her feet in her long night gown
To make a little joke you won't have the taste
When you take a peep at her jaguar face
If you want trouble and misery
Give an ugly woman matrimony

Winston: I don't know if how a woman look all that important.

Saga: Country, what you know not important. You did
know nothing before last night, and what you
know now is nothing special. 'Love me or leave
me'? That heat wouldn't outlast a night.

Radio: *(Enters with Pa Gomes)* Heroes! We back on the
field of battle!

Battler: You get the licence?

Radio: Forget 'bout licence! I talking now about the future of calypso! This, heroes, is Pa Gomes, businessman and proprietor of Frederick Street. Pa, tell them what you say to me as I passing your store this morning on my way to the Police Constabulary.

Gomes: Gentlemen, the Decca Company of New York, is interested in making recordings of Trinidad calypso. They've asked me to select the best calypsonians to send to New York.

Battler: You mean America?

Radio: How much New York it have? All you hear the man? You know what that mean? We calypso on record just like Rudy Vallee, Bing Crosby! The world waiting on we song!

Saga: That mean money in we pocket. They have to pay we for we songs, not so, Pa Gomes?

Gomes: Of course. The rate will be $10.00 a song. But that's only for the best.

Battler: Ten whole dollars!

Gomes: Plus your passage to New York, of course.

Saga: When we starting, Pa Gomes?

Timer: Mr. Gomes, if you don't mind, how come Decca choose you to conduct this business?

Radio: How you mean, Timer? Pa Gomes have big business connections all over the place.

Gomes: Let's say, it's a collaboration of interests. Including the calypsonians.

Timer: And how you plan to select the best calypsonians, Mr. Gomes?

Radio: Timer always asking some damn fool question. Like you getting dotish with age? It must be the king of the tent that get pick first. Not so, Pa?

Gomes: Well, I'm more interested in the calypso than the calypsonian. If the people like a song and it's a hit, then the record should sell well. That's the way I'm seeing it. You boys better get on the move. Destination U.S.A. *(Waves goodbye. Exits)*

Saga: Imagine. Mighty Saga stepping off this ocean liner in fine style, dressed to kill and waltzing through New York not without a bevy of beauties in train, which one to shine his shoes, which one to comb his hair, which one to keep the fans at bay. I enter the studio.......

Radio: And have to wait in line, because the masters of the art already in there recording! Atilla!

Timer: (GRAF ZEPPELIN)
One Sunday morning I chanced to hear
A rumbling and a tumbling in the atmosphere}Repeat
I ran to stare, people were flocking everywhere
Gesticulating and gazing and pointing in the air
It was the Graf Zeppelin that had
Come to pay a visit to Trinidad

I gazed at the Zeppelin contemplatively
And marvelled at man's ingenuity

The whirring of the engine was all I heard
As it floated in the air like some giant bird
And in between as the mighty airship leaned
The pilots and the sailors and the passengers
were seen
They were waving little flags which they had
Heralding their visit to Trinidad

I gazed and the knowledge came back to me
How wonderful the work of man can be
To see that huge object in the air
Maintaining perfect equilibrium in the atmosphere
Wonderfully, beautifully, gloriously
Decidedly defying all the laws of gravity
Was the Graf Zeppelin which had
Come to pay a visit to Trinidad

Radio: The Growler!

Winston: (DEW AND RAIN)

Chorus:

In the dew and the rain, everybody
In the dew and the rain
All over Port of Spain
I mean they only walking in vain

At the corner of George and Prince Street at night
When the tents are closed in the midst a fight
You can see them sitting down in the dew
I don't know how the france they don't catch the flu

And when they get no living
To hear them friends how they quarreling

Woe be on to the man that make a mistake
For even his gold and all they will take
Oh well they drink they gamble, they smoke
To pick seamen pockets, friends it's a joke
And daily they are throwing down the young lads
And blighting the island of Trinidad

Now this is my third anniversary
Singing on the rats in this colony
I know they all are angry with me
But daily they are gaining humanity.

Radio: (HISTORY OF CARNIVAL)
From a scandal and hideous bacchanal}
Today we got a glorious carnival} repeat
We used to sing long ago

Nou ni yo
Plein pou sein ne yo
But today you can hear our calypso
On the American radio

Carnival of long ago you used to see
Half naked woman called the pis en lit
With shack-shack and vira in they hand
Twisting they body as electric fan
You were not safe in your home
From the neg jardin with bottle and stone
But today you can hear our calypso
On the American radio

Some of the songsters I can remember
Were Malborough and Executor
Black Prince, Pharaoh and Fijonel
Edward the Confessor whom I knew well

They used to sing mama mouni yo
Captain Baker was a whoopster, I don't know
(vi yo glo)
But today you can hear our calypso
On the American radio

Carnival of long ago was real terrible
And the orgies reprehensible
In those days women sang calypsoes
Like Sophie Mataloney and Maribo
They used to walk bout with boul de fe
In the days of the Canboulay
But today you can hear our calypso
On the American radio

A prophet has no honour in his own land
The truth of that proverb I now understand
When you sing calypso in Trinidad
You're a vagabond and everything that's bad
In your native land you're a hooligan
In New York you're an artist and gentleman
For instance take the Lion and me
Having dinner with Rudy Vallee.

Saga: I can't wait on all you, nuh. I going and change my
clothes and head down one time by Pa Gomes.
New York? I ain't missing *(Exits to room)*
that boat.

Battler: Me neither. Dorothy go have to look out for
sheself. *(Goes in)*

Radio: All you do fast.

Timer: You not anxious too, Wonderboy? Is New York,
you know.

Winston:	I know I good but look at the names in the race - Atilla, Lion, Tiger, Growler, and Radio, heself. Them is the giants of the art.
Timer:	What is for you is for you. Nobody could thief your luck.
Saga:	*(Rushing out of room)* Matilda! That bitch!
Timer:	What happen, boy?
Saga:	That damn woman! You know what she do? *(All now outside)*
Battler:	She ain't finish cook?
Radio:	What happen? She ain't iron your clothes?
Saga:	Me money! The damn woman thief me money and gone!
Louise:	You mean...the money you had stash way for the two of we?
Radio:	You sure, boy? Where she gone?
Battler:	By the seamstress, she say.
Timer:	So she say.
Saga:	O God, and I did hide that money so good, O God!
Radio:	*(To audience)* So where she gone? Where she really gone? (MATILDA)

Chorus:
Matilda, Matilda, Matilda
You take me money and run Venezuela

It really hurt me friends but what to do
Listen how the woman draft a screw
Never me friends to love again
Now listen how me money gone in vain

Five thousand dollars, friends I loss
The woman even sell me cart and horse

Me money was to buy a house and land
Now listen how she draft a serious plan

The money was quite below me bed
Chooke-up in me mattress, right below me head

Ah feel a jumbie touch me head
He say boy no money inside the bed

When I jook me hand was all in vain
Right on the spot, I touch cellophane

(They exit to the street with this lavway)

Act 2

Scene I

Saga: *(A dejected figure after his abandonment by Matilda and failure to obtain work)*
(PARAMARIBO)
Chorus:
Paramaribo

That's the place I want to go
I am such a crooked lad
I can't find work in Trinidad

I tried all technological screws
But was kept back by circumstantial abuse
I can't eliminate the discrepancies
It unfortunately brings to my family

Indescribable unsuccessfulness
Patience is virtue but I can't bear this
Sweet are the uses of adversity
A proverb for the rich ones but not for me

My incessant endeavours constantly fail
By entirely producing the saddest tale
But if I can't get money today
I will pay rat passage and stow away

Looking back at those dependant on me
House rent to pay and a young baby
A sick wife, four children, a mother-in-law
Incessant appeals make my heart more sore

Sometimes when hunger stares me in my face
Not even a slice of mango to taste
Don't you think it's a mortal sin
For me to be daily living on wind

My clothes is tattered my shoes is bad
Friends is not my biology sad
My children is naked, hungry and pale
I'm blest that I've not yet been sent to jail

But in spite of all my desolation
I've evaded all evil inspiration

I'm taking a chance although it is bad
I'm compulsory bound to leave Trinidad.

Timer: *(Comments on what he reads in the newspaper)*
THE GOLD IN AFRICA

Chorus:
The gold, the gold, the gold, the gold,
The gold in Africa
Mussolini want from the Emperor

Abyssinia appeal to the League for peace
Mussolini's action was like a beast
A villain, a thief, a highway robber
And a shameless dog for a dictator

Chorus

He crossed the border and added more
The Emperor had no intention for war
That man I call a criminal
The man destroyed churches and hospitals

Chorus

He said expansion he really need
He had forty-five million heads to feed
Why he don't attack the Japanese
England, France or hang on, on Germany

Chorus

The man want to kill King Haile Selassie
To enslave his territory
They began to cry for food and water
In that burning desert of Africa

Chorus

We have diamonds, rubies and pearls
Platinum, silver and even gold
I don't know why the man making so much strife
I now believe he want Haile Selassie wife

Chorus

If you want gold as dictator
Try in Demerara, Venezuela or Canada
Austria-Hungary or else in America

Winston: *(As crowd changes into a workers' march)*
(WORKERS' PLEA)
Anywhere you go you must meet people sad }
They search for employment none can be had} repeat
They start to drop down dead in the street
Nothing to eat and no where to sleep
All kind hearted employers I appeal now to you
Give us some work to do

We are not asking for equality
To rank with the rich in society
To visit their homes in their motor car
Or to go their clubs and smoke their cigars
We are asking for a living wage
To help us now and provide for old age
All kind hearted employers I appeal now to you
Give us some work to do

Many a day folks who haven't a meal
They were too decent to beg, to honest to steal
They went looking for work mostly everywhere
 But all sign boards mark 'no hands wanted here'
The Government should work the wastelands
and hills

Build houses factories and mills
Reduce taxation and then we would be really
Emancipated from slavery

The legislators only quarrel and fret
About unemployment but haven't relieved us yet
There is no vision that we can see
To take us out from tribulations and misery
We can't fight physically cause we wouldn't prevail
On account of ammunition cruel laws and jail
But every man was born to be free from this oppression
And tyrannic slavery.

(Inset: Meanwhile at the Country club, the Inspector General of Police and the owner of the Port of Spain Gazette 'the grand old Lady of Port of Spain'.)

Grand: It's been agreed that we raise the worker's pay, darling.

Inspector: Backbone, that's what your colonial employer lacks. How much?

Grand: Quite substantial, I'm afraid. Four cents a day.

Inspector: Now that's ridiculous! How will we ever maintain law and order in the colony when employers bow to every absurd demand by the workers? And it's getting worse. Look at the kind of stuff they're singing *(Showing censored material)* 'Why doesn't Mussolini attack England or France', for instance. More than a hint of sedition there! Here again, We don't want to smoke your cigars or drive in your expensive motorcars! You see? It's saying what it's not saying! There's a word for that...

Grand: Irony?

Inspector: Innuendo?

Grand: Double entendre?

Inspector: Damned dangerous! Then there's the other type.

Grand: *(Quizzical)*

Inspector: You know. *(Shows her a line or two)*

Grand: *(Reads)* Nettie, Nettie, gimme the thing that you got in your belly.Óh, dear!

Inspector: Lewd, isn't it?

Grand: I just wish they'd speak properly. The grammar's awful.

Inspector: The entire thing's objectionable, I daresay. And those devils with the collusion of one of your local businessmen had them recorded.

Grand: Well? What will you do with them?

Inspector: Will? As the records arrived on the docks this morning I had them all dumped.

Grand: Dumped?

Inspector: Exactly so. In the Gulf of Paria.

Grand: *(Pause)* Well, there's an end to that. Poor boy, poor Inspector General. You take your job too seriously.

Inspector: I'm a serious man, dear Port of Spain Gazette. I'm serious about you.

(They embrace passionately. Suddenly he stiffens)

Grand: What is it? What's the matter, you naughty boy?

Inspector: Your husband.

(Crowd resumes demonstration)

Winston: (TRY A SCREW)
The government should really
deal more leniently   }
With the unemployed of this colony   } repeat
Work no where, I mean you have a rent to pay
The money population is decreasing every day
After all there's no work to do
We bound to try a screw to get through

You may look for work it's natural of course
But if your money finish you have no resource
It's the bigshot man who must thrive alone
How must we live on a bed of stone
You'll have to play wappie dice or rummy
Or take a hand in necromancy
Open your brain if you can make money
Or join the chain of burglary

It only needs a little observation
To notice the change in this Iere land
Mango crop we can hardly see
 Breadfruit gone out entirely
Cassava you does see now and again
Everything does turn up on the poor sugar cane
After all there's no work to do
We bound to try a screw to get through

An old man told me one day quite plain
When I was going to the city on the midday train

When he was a boy in 1894
He was king to the boys who were naked and poor
I knew a boy who played Hawaiian music in his nose
One had a bottle as a bass seventh note
After all there's no work to do
They bound to try a screw to get through

College youths used to walk into Toco Bay
Wearing their shoes, can't get work today
With all their education, some bite their nails
Play wey-wey, break shop or live in jail
Is rather hard in this land of Trinidad
The living conditions is enough to drive us mad
After all there's no work to do
We bound to try a screw to get through.

Louise: You neck and neck with that madman. Watch yourself, you know, Winston.

Winston: And then what? How long I must sit down watching myself and things going from bad to worse?

Timer: *(Reading)* Papers calling it the Great Depression. All over the world people catching hell.

Winston: Not like down here. We have no say, so for we it worse. Radio lucky . He stay out.

Louise: Saga first, then Radio. Nothing is the same. I even miss the lil busing with Saga on a morning.

Timer: Hmm! Big meeting tonight. Tubal Uriah Buzz Butler.

Dorothy: *(Entering from street)* Eh bien! If you see that line! Two hours it take me to reach the counter and when I get there this short-arse Chinaman saying no pitch-oil and I could only get two pounds of flour. Two pounds, when I have to eat and bake my lil sweetbread to sell!

Louise: But like you get more than that girl.

Dorothy: I tell him don't bother with my ration card, watch my size good. When he done watch me he ask if ten pounds is all I want.

Winston: Starvation in the land, Madame Khan.

Dorothy: Not for everybody.

(BLACK MARKET)
I see the black market}
Is making a big hit} repeat
Some people doing well
While others are catching hell
Only black market have me blue
But I bound to jump in it too.

The paper sensation
Sign the pledge for protection
Everybody went madly
But they never went to it truly
While they taking the pen to sign
The black market was on their minds
Even racketeers use it too
For they run and sign it up too

Those who doing well is shopkeepers
Provision and wholesale dealers
They have no worries for Hitler
They have everything to their leisure
All they friends does be treated right

They does get their parcels at night
So I ask them to go and see
How some people house like a grocery

I say the cost of living is rising
With the goods its surprising
But I haven't no money
And the things looking funny
I went to shop with schedule price
And the Chinee man say no rice
If I play I going for real schedule
I will starve and die like a fool

Winston: Even in the tent. People can't fork out the four
cents these nights to hear good kaiso. So I singing
where the people is. With Butler.

Louise: You just be careful.

Dorothy: And you, Mr. Battler, get up and come outside.   I
leave you sleeping and come back and find you
sleeping while I out catching my nen-nen to find
food for you to gobble? Louise, a lazy man does
blight your life.

Louise: At least you know where Battler does be.

Timer: Everybody have they cross to bear.

**Louise/
Dorothy:**   Who talk to you?

Battler: *(Emerging)* W'happen? What I do now?

Dorothy: Nutten. And that is just the point. Breadline for
days, salt and all is black market, and you not doing
one damn thing.

Battler: I ain't have no work. What you want me to do?

Dorothy: Go and tell the Government you want a work.
Demand one! Tell them that you Ignatius John is a
born Trinidadian and no Chinee shopkeeper could
tell you how much flour to buy!

Battler: What flour have to do with it?

Dorothy: Don't ask stupidness! If you was alive to the world
you would know. Go with Winston and see how
other men demanding their rights.

Battler: Alright, alright, don't raise your hand.

Dorothy: Go on. I tired tell you I ain't minding no lazy man!

Battler: Alright. Lemme take a lil breakfast before...

Dorothy: Breakfast? You really looking for me to scramble
your eggs today or what?

Battler: I gone, I gone. *(Outside of room)* You ever see a
love like that? Mornin' Miss Louise. Aye, Winston,
I think I liming with you today, yes.

Winston: No problem. You have tram-fare?

Battler: For one. Where we going?

Winston: Fyzabad. To the Butler meeting.

Battler: Fyza-who?

Winston: *(As crowd gathers for Butler meeting)*
(MONEY IS KING)

If a man have money today   }
People do not care if he have cocobay } repeat
 He can commit murder and get off free
And live in the Governor's company
But if you are poor, people will tell you shoo
And a dog is better than you

If you have money to buy in a store
The boss will shake your hands at the door
Call them clerk to take down everything
Whiskey, cloth, ear-ring and diamond ring
Send them to your house on a motor-bike
You can pay the bills whenever you like
Not a soul will ask you a thing
They know very well that money is king

A man with collar, tie and waistcoat
Ask a Chinaman to trust him accra and float
Me no trust am bawl out the Chinaman
And you better move am from me frying pan
You college man, me know no a,b,c
You want am accra gie am penny
The worms start to jump in the man belly
And he cried out a dog is better than me

A dog can walk bout and pick up bone
Fowl head, stale bread, fish tail and pone
If it's a good breed and not too wild
People will take it and mind as a child
But when a hungry man goes out to beg
They will set a bull dog behind his leg
Forty policemen will chock him down too
So you see where a dog is better than you

If you have money and things going nice
Any woman would call you honey and spice

If you can't give her a dress or a new pair of shoes
She'll say she have no uses for you
Try to caress her she will tell you stop
I can't carry love in the Chinee shop
I'm sure most of you will agree that is true
If you haven't money, dog is better than you.

Butler: *(Addresses crowd)*
(FOUR CENTS A DAY) *(spoken)*
Four cents a day
That's what they put on worker's pay
I would say it again I don't know who is to blame
But it is a burning shame
No wonder people through hunger and discontent
Are saying we have a criminal government.

I am calling on every authority
To look into this matter carefully
And make some decent effort to give
The worker a wage on which he can live
He don't want no ivory bars, or to drive in motorcars
Or smoke expensive cigars
All that he wants is a guarantee
To be able to provide for his family

An Englishman came here recently
And started to grumble about his salary
Two hundred dollars a month he told them flat
With the cost of living he couldn't exist on that
He resigned with regret now his salary don't forget
Is more than what twenty workers get
And still they want them to be happy and gay
On the princely raise of four cents a day

I went to the Square just the other day
And what I saw filled me with dismay
It stands out in my memory

As a demonstration of sheer brutality
Workers were walking around
When near the Red House they were found
Starving people begging for bread
We offer them tear gas and lead instead.

Santapee: *(Makes his way through the audience)*
Tubal Uriah Buzz Butler! Tell the people go home.
Is you I want.

Butler: Look, the police send their santapee to arrest me!

Santapee: Break this up! Break this up! All you go home!
(Takes hold of Butler)

Butler: You people will let this santapee take the Chief
Servant?

Crowd: No! No! Don't touch him!

Santapee: Any trouble and is shooting tonight! I have orders
to fire!

Butler: The santapee ready to fire! But we know what we
does do with santapee!

Crowd: Fire! Fire!

Santapee: *(As they crowd him, lets go of Butler, runs. The women pursue
him. He leaps from a height and falls breaking his legs).
The women converge above. Shouts from the Inspector-
general in background of 'Fire'. The women work almost
instinctively, a scene rehearsed in their loins. A can of pitch-
oil is poured on the lame, groaning figure below.
A light is thrown. Screams. The women dance fire
as their men fight and fall and the figure writhes
to a blazing stop.*

Women: (MAN SANTAPEE)

Chorus:
Man santapee bad, bad
But woman santapee more than bad
Man santapee bad, bad
But woman santapee more than bad

Winston: (*As he is beaten by police and placed in prison*)
(IN MY OWN NATIVE LAND)
Ah mwen pa sa dormi comme mwen vle
(I cannot sleep as I want)
Ah mwen pa ca marche comme mwen vle
(I cannot walk about as I want)
Ah mwen pa ca couche comme mwen vle
(I cannot lie down where I want)
Mwen vle pon couche comme mwen vle
(I want to lie down where I want)
Mwen vle pou dormi comme mwen ye
(I want to sleep as I am)

Timer: (SEDITION LAW)
Believe I warning the rich and poor
Be careful friends today from this Sedition Law
If you charge with that offence you have no evidence
They mean to license we mouth
They don't want we talk
Ya de ya, ya de oo

A fellar was charged for that offence
And his lawyer couldn't break down the evidence
It was the jurors decision that he was guilty
But the judge really acted with sympathy
I mean by giving him two years in custody
Ya de yo, ya dee oo

They mean to licence we mouth
They don't want we talk

Agree with any man who speaking for their rights
But you cannot say everything what you like
There's certain things would affect the authorities
Who has the strength and the force in this colony
And when you get the blow, in the jail you walk
Ya de ya, ya de oo

You want to be versed in politics
I mean you got to be lucky with lots of tricks
First you got to use a little diplomacy
Mix up with common sense and psychology
And when you get the blow - not only talk
They mean to license we foot
They don't want we walk
Ya de ya, ya de oo

Politics improve in our native land
Being lectured and preached by women and men
You got to know friends what you talking about
Else you sure to pay damn dear for your mouth
So if you know you can't use the knife and fork
They mean to license we mouth
They don't want we talk
Ya de ya, ya de oo

Winston, boy, you earn your name fighting for the
people's sake. No more Siparia Kid, no more
Wonderboy. From today, call yourself the Mighty
Crusader. May your sword remain high in the cause
of kaiso!

Inspector
Gen.
& Grand
Old Lady: *Draw curtains across the act*

Act 3 *(Two Years Later)*

Theme: *Rum and Coca Cola. Much bustle as yard is converted into a U.S. 'Entertainment Center' with buntings, posters, etc.)*

Winston: *(Enters from street)*

Battler: Aye, no liming! If you ain't have money in your pocket, move off. Here is $10.00 up.

Winston: Battler?

Battler: Who is that? Crusader? You out, boy! Two years pass real fast!

Winston: Time. I was wondering if I in the right place.

Battler: Everything change up, boy. With the War the whole world change, so who is we, eh? This ain't La Cou Kaiso no more. You standing in the Bonanza Entertainment Center!

Winston: That is what the sign say. But why?

Battler: The Americans, boy. 'Tent' to them is something to spread out and camp in. The word just don't make no sense to them and is them that paying the piper these days.

Winston: Even inside the talk is the Yankee dollar.

Battler: Kaiso is big money now. The Yanks paying $5.00 to $7.00 a night to hear any old thing. You come back in good time.

Winston: Louise?

Battler: Alright, man. Even the Madame join in the action. She move out and set up she own place in St. James. Down there business even better!

Winston: We'll talk later. *(Moving toward Louise's room)*

Battler: Aye, Crusader, how come you ain't ask for your ol pardner?

Winston: Who is that?

Battler: Timer, nuh. Who else?

Winston: Well?

Battler: Time catch up with him. *(Laughs)*

Sailors: *(With girls swaying drunkenly into yard)*
'Rum and Coca Cola
Go down Pt. Cumana
Both mother and daughter
Working for the Yankee dollar'

Sailor I: That's how it goes, Battler?

Sailor II: Who the hell cares?

Battler: That's it, Joe. You got it. See what I tell you, Crusader?

Winston: See you later, Battler.

Battler: You can't go in there.

Winston: What the hell you mean, man?

(Door opens. Louise with Saga)

Louise: Hi, Winston.

Saga: That's how you greet your ex-lover? 'Hi, Winston?' Shame on you, girl. Go greet the man properly.

Battler: I tried to keep him out, Saga.

Saga: Forget it, Battler. You was never much good at nothing. So Crusader, you at a loss for words or what? You look alright. Jail suit you.

Winston: Hi, Louise. *(Silence)*

Saga: Some reunion. Battler, bring a bottle. Let's celebrate the man's return. Hey, what you think of the spread though? My Bonanza Entertainment Center?

Winston: Yours?

Saga Sure, baby. Didn't do so badly when I left here. Moved on from Paramaribo to the U.S. Calypso King up there. Couple of good deals, some luck, some plain Trinidadian home sense and here I am. I own it all. Let's take a drink.

Winston: Lost the habit. Louise, let's talk.

Saga: Hey, don't you get the picture, man?

Louise: Is alright, Saga. I want to hear what he have to say.

Saga: Whatever you say, babes. Just remember, you got company tonight. *(Moves aside)*

Battler: (RUM AND COCA COLA) *(Background)*

Louise: It didn't make sense, Winston. Two years was too long.

Winston: I could understand that. But to whore!

Louise: Watch your words with me, Winston. I pick and choose as always. You forget how you get into that room.

Winston: I didn't buy you, girl. You tell me love you or leave you and I put my bag down.

Louise: Empty, or you forget that too? I don't have no excuse. I don't need none. What I do now is just like before. Only this time the men pay.

Winston: Lord, why my sentence wasn't ten, twenty years, til this nightmare pass?

Louise: A hundred years wouldn't be long enough. Wake up, Winston. This is the real world, we world now.

Winston: The 'Bonanza Entertainment Center'?
No! Never!

Saga: You o.k., Lou?

Louise: Sure, Saga.

Winston: 'Sure, Saga'. You turn Yankee and all.

Louise: I just accept change, Winston. Is change you was fighting for on the Butler platform.

Winston: You didn't understand then and you still can't see now. Wasn't change I sing for or make this jail for,

that so many die for. Was betterment.
Not no 'Bonanza Entertainment Center' whore-
house.

Saga: Time, Lou.

Louise: Look, I got to go, but hold this till you get on your
feet.

Winston: Keep your stinking, whoring money!

Saga: Aye, buddy, none of that in here! I run a straight
establishment. You don't like it, you go elsewhere,
but no messing around with my investment, damn it!
(pause) You o.k., Lou?

Louise: I'm fine, Saga. See you around, Winston.

Battler: (LOUISE) *In background*

Saga: Look, buddy, I know how it feels. I lost a woman in
this yard too, remember? Didn't show it then, but it
hurt no bitch. I put that behind me and here I am
now. Time. *(Pause)* Tell you what, you wasn't a bad
calypsonian. With all them new tents around, you'd
make a difference to my team. Why not come on
the show tonight. Earn some good money.

Winston: You can't buy me, Saga. I ain't Battler.

Saga: Hell, I couldn't afford to. I ain't that loaded. Look,
get smart. You just out and you need money. Ain't
my money, it's the Yanks'. They willing to
pay, why the hell not take it? *(Pause)* Well, it's an
invitation. Show starts at 8:00p.m. sharp.

Battler: (LOUISE) (*Joined by* Saga)
Louise, hope is not in vain
Please come back again
Louise, hope is not in vain
Please come back again
Miss your romance when you leave
Miss your bliss I had to grieve
Oh girl look I now realise that I lost my paradise

Chorus:
Darling, doo doo
Why you make me blue, oh girl
Everytime I turn in me bed
I take the pillow for you

Darling, do you wonder why
Sweet love could never die
Louise, girl I must confess
Your love is of the best
You could bring a lion just like a lamb
You're got something that could really charm
Oh girl I now realise that I lost my paradise

Louise, speaking broad-mindedly
You just like a honey bee
Oh, with the dames I know
None ever thrill me so
I love to hear your happy tones
Retaliate with the things you own
O girl, look I now realise that I lost my paradise

Louise, telling you candidly
You got something holding me
Oh, what it is at all
That make me have to bawl

Bring it back, I'm paralysed
For you've got me victimized
Oh girl, look I now realise that I lost my paradise.

**Inspector-
Gen:**

Ladies and gentlemen, I am indeed grateful to the
management of this er....pub, the Bonanza Entertainment Center, for taking a few minutes off its
quite splendid show for this patriotic announce-
ment. I want to exhort you, on behalf of Her
Majesty's Government, to use this absolutely
wonderful instrument, your calypso, in the Allied
cause. As you know we have always stood behind
you and I have no doubt that as loyal
and patriotic citizens of the Crown you will
continue to do all you can to add to the comfort,
welfare and morale of the troops stationed here.
Thank you and may I make a special request for
that absolutely superb little ditty, 'Adolf Hitler'.

Saga:

(ADOLF HITLER)
Adolf Hitler, Adolf Hitler
How you looking at the British Empire
Adolf Hitler, Adolf Hitler
How you looking at the British Empire
You planned an invasion
You must be taking Britain for Poland
But you'll be a failure
Britain is supported by America

Yes, you wanted war what you fighting for
You got expansion and you still demanding more
You took Austria, Czechoslovakia
And now you grasping at the British Empire
France capitulated

And in the same way is Belgium situated
But you must surrender
Britain is supported by America

Napoleon Bonaparte had a better start
But the crossing of the Channel broke his heart
1636 the Spaniards tried their tricks
But they also were defeated with plenty licks
You Austrian jailbird
These are things in history you're never heard
So I must remind you
The whole world respects the red, white and blue

Our Prime Minister, Churchill your master
Said it wouldn't take you long to surrender
The Kaiser's intention of world domination
Had him in Holland paying retribution
Your friend Mussolini
Through the Greeks he bound to lose Italy
And by this and summer
We have him like Napoleon on St. Helena.

I don't know about you but I say 'God bless
America'. If wasn't for the U.S., Hitler would be in
Port of Spain already and we would have to learn to
sing calypso in German. America's done wonders
for the artform too. Friend of mine, Morey
Amsterdam took one of our calypsoes back to the
U.S., the Andrew Sisters recorded it and its making
millions for them. Tonight as a special treat, we
present a version of the Andrews Sister's version of
Lord Invader's ever-popular 'Rum and Coca Cola'.

(Male Chorus in drag) (RUM AND COCA COLA)
(Andrew's Sisters' version)

Chorus: If you ever go down Trinidad
They make you feel so very glad
Calypso sing and make up rhyme
Guarantee you one real, good, fine time

Chorus

Drinking rum and coco cola
Go down Point Cumana
Both mother and daughter
Working for the yankee dollar

Since the yankee come to Trinidad
They got the young girls all going mad
Young girls say they treat them nice
Make Trinidad like paradise

From Chikichicare to Monas Isle
The native girls all dance and smile
Help soldier celebrate his leave
Make every day like New Year's Eve

In all Trinidad I also hear
The situation is mighty queer
Like Yankee girls and natives swoon
When she hears De Bingo croon

Out on Manzanilla beach
G.I.'s romance the native peach
All night long make tropic love
Next day sit in hot sun and cool off

Saga: Back on the scene tonight, ladies and gentlemen, is
a voice well known before the War. Together, we
go back to the days, before I became Calypso King

of the whole United States, when he came green as
a country guana and I it was, who guided and
encouraged him to enter calypso. I even
christened him in the calypso world. Ladies and
gentleman, a calypsonian of conscience and one
always with the people's interest close to his heart,
the Mighty Crusader!

Winston: (LET THE WHITE PEOPLE FIGHT)
Times so hard you cannot deny
Even saltfish and rice I can hardly buy
Times so hard you cannot deny
Even saltfish and rice I can hardly buy
As the war declare with England and Germany
I can't drink a little bit of milk in me tea
But I would plant provision and fix my affairs
And let the war continue fighting ten thousand years

Before the war I was living nice
Crush potato with my bacon, stew pork and rice
Toast bread with butter and jam
Seven eggs in the morning, big junks of ham
Today I living like a wandering bird
If I see the pot for seconds, I can't find the food
I living by guess so have sympathy
Since the war declare with England and Germany

I am so hard-pressed in this colony
That the stores refuse to sell a suit of khaki
Me boot sole gone, it twist on the side
With all this prostitution I must abide
If I have a cigarette I can't find a match
I can't trim me hair, I wearing saddle patch
My shirt and my jacket start turning green
Since Hitler the pressure to man intervene

But I want a piece of land at Mt. Hololo
So I could plant me dasheen, fig and ochro
I looking at this thing as a mortal sin
Condense milk selling fourteen cents a tin
I go give them a fall with me limes you see
And if they bring it two dollars it doh worry me
I going to plant provision and fix my affairs
And let the white people fight for ten thousand
years

The only thing that worrying me
Is the ship with the food from the open sea
Friends they nearly kill *(Crusader)*
With that arsenic product from Demerara
It appears as if me next door neighbour get bad
Demerara declare war on Trinidad
But I will plant provision and fix my affairs
And let the people continue fighting ten thousand
years.

(At end of song) Ladies and gentlemen, so much
change happen to this yard, this land since I last sing
on a stage, that though I still young, I feel like a real
old timer. Is not easy and I can't say I like what I
see and hear, but friends, all the more reason to sing.
How else will our story be told? I singing of the
greats of the past - Executor, Atilla, Lion, Radio,
Tiger, Growler, Destroyer and Timer - and for
whatever tomorrow may bring.

Louise: You forgetting one Lady Iere, or you don't think
women could be great too?

Louise: (WHICH IS THE BEST)
O lovely woman or noble man   }
Which is the best of creation's plan   } repeat

The heart of a man a woman can hold
When men are fearless, noble and bold
So we will put it to the test
Then one will confess
To find out which is the best

I can show you in a simple way
Where women the best parts they always play
In the war with canons, bayonets and guns
They all did their parts and they did not run
While men were falling down everywhere
As Red Cross nurses, these men they did care
So let us put it to the test
And one will confess
To find out which is the best.

Winston: The onliest thing that a man can't do
Is to put life in both I and you
Men first went thousands of feet in the air
All through the clouds and the atmosphere
Women were made for men to control
Therefore men were meant to govern this world
So if you put it to the test
You bound to confess
That man is by far the best

Let me make you to understand
No woman more noble than man
A man can make, a man can break
A man can shake just like an earthquake

Louise: But when a woman set out for you
Say what you want you cannot get through

**Louise/
Winston:** So let us put it to the test
And we will confess

That both of them is the best.
(They smile at each other)

Town Rat: Aye! A whole side a fellas set up a tent in Edward
Street. If you see people!

Saga: Who they is?

Town Rat: Names that don't mean nothing - Spoiler,
Wonder, Killer. It even have one calling heself
Kitchener.

Battler: Kitchener? He come to wash wares.

Winston: No genealogy.

Town Rat: But people love them though. They calling theyself
the Young Brigade and they waiting, battle-ready,
they say to tackle the Bonanza Timers.

Winston: I ain't know 'bout Saga with all this American thing,
nuh, but you could tell them the Mighty Crusader
coming to show them what is true, true kaiso!

Saga: What American thing, you talking 'bout, man? Up
there was easy pickings. This is the real battlefield.
Tell them is Saga on the road, a born kaisonian!
Folks, excuse but you understand, a call to battle.

Winston: Sing de Chorus!

All: (SING DE CHORUS)

(Exeunt)

Ah Wanna Fall

(Calypsoes of the post war era)

Characters

FIGSKIN /BROTHER WILLIE

MING / PROSECUTOR

RIBERO/ MAGISTRATE

GAZA / CHORUS

SPOILER

IMELDA DARLING / CHORUS

KITCHENER

POPO

TINA

TOURIST I /MISS PRIM /CHORUS

TOURIST 2 / CHORUS

TOURIST 3 / MACO MAISIE /CHORUS

DRIVER / CHIN / BOLT

CONSTABLE 1 / CHORUS

SALES

CONSTABLE 2 / CHORUS

Ah Wanna Fall was first produced by Canboulay Productions in January 1992. The production was directed by Louis McWilliams with the following cast:

FIGSKIN /BROTHER WILLIE- Leon Roach
MING / LORD BLAKIE- Paul Guerra
RIBERO/ MAGISTRATE- Errol Jones
GAZA / CHORUS- Ucill Cambridge
SPOILER- David Bereaux
IMELDA DARLING / CHORUS- Denise Atherly
KITCHENER- Clem Haynes
POPO- Rhoma Spencer
TINA- Helen Williams
TOURIST I /MISS PRIM /CHORUS- Mary Jack
TOURIST 2 / CHORUS- Sharon Devenish
TOURIST 3 / MACO MAISIE /CHORUS- Leah Gordon
DRIVER / CHIN / BOLT- Michael Cherrie
CONSTABLE 1 / CHORUS- Kurtis Gross
SALES- Christopher Sheppard
CONSTABLE 2 / CHORUS - David Scobie
PROSECUTOR / CHORUS- Derrek Casanova
CHORUS- Kandissan Harry

Musicians

MUSICAL DIRECTOR/ CUATRO- Desmond Waithe
GUITAR- Marva Newton
FLUTE /TROMBONE- Cuthbert Fletcher
BASS- Alisford Phillips
TRUMPET- Vernon Matthews
PIANO- Dennis Kadan
DRUMS- Odilia Garcia, Louis McWilliams

List Of Calypsoes

PROFESSOR KITCHENER-Lord Kitchener
YOUNG BRIGADE-Theme Song
TIE-TONGUE MOPSEY-Lord Kitchener
MAN IN THE WARDROBE-Lord Kitchener
ALL FOOLS' DAY-Spoiler
FOUNTAIN OF YOUTH-Spoiler
FATHER CHRISTMAS-Spoiler
OL' LADY WALK A MILE-Lord Kitchener
DEATH IS COMPULSORY-Lord Kitchener
NYLON MAN-Wonder
TAXI-DRIVER-Panther
CONSTABLE JOE-Lord Kitchener
V.J. DAY-Lord Kitchener
CHINESE CRICKET MATCH-Dictator
WENT TO COLLEGE-Spoiler
HINDU WEDDING-Killer
FOLLOW ME CHILDREN-Wonder
WORLD OF TOMMOROW-Spoiler
SUGAR BUM BUM-Lord Kitchener
WOMAN POLICE-Spoiler
TWIN BROTHER-Spoiler
MY WIFE GONE-Lord Kitchener
UGLY AS SIN-Wonder
PORTUGUESE DANCE-Pharoah
TALKING BACKWARD-Spoiler
MONEY IN THE BANK-Spoiler
RAMGOAT BAPTISM-Wonder
STEELBAND CLASH-Lord Blakie
OL' TIME CAT O' NINE-Lord Invader
NO CRIME NO LAW-Commander
MAGISTRATE TRY HIMSELF-Spoiler
CAT BRAIN-Spoiler
GLORY MAMA GLORY-Melody
JUST DEY-Panther

NEVER WORRY-Pretender
DIESEL LADY SHAW-Wonder
AH BERNICE-Lord Kitchener
CAKE STICKING-Spoiler
RUM BACCHANAL-Spoiler
LAST TRAIN-Duke Of Iron
MY SHADOW-Spoiler
GREEN FOWL-Killer
MR. ACTION-Commander
TOCO WAKE-Wonder
BEDBUG-Spoiler

Act 1

Scene I

Darkness, in a tight spot Kitch sings:
(PROFESSOR KITCHENER)

I am giving my opinion candidly
About calypso singers and their ability
The Spoiler for ideas he is the best
And by a long long way he surpass the rest
Melody is clever in his bounce and tune
And I really like to hear the way that mister croon
But calypso wouldn't be complete so far
If you leave out the Professor Lord Kitchener

Lord Pretender the whole world know
He is the master of them all in extempo
The Skipper is good as a musician
I also recommend his composition
For real jocular singing Viking is my choice
And we can't ignore the Terror the man with the voice

But calypso won't be complete so far
If you leave out the Professor Lord Kitchener

The Young Kitchener, that singing bird
He is the best renderer I have ever heard
And for popular singers, you all should know
Pride, Zebra, Dictator, and King Pharaoh
The Wonder and the Zigfield they come poke a poke
At times when they are singing they may crack a joke
But calypso won't be complete so far
If you leave out the Professor, Lord Kitchener

Last but not least, this I have to say
It shock me when I heard Killer pass away
A great entertainer in every case
A singer that we can hardly replace
When he sang that murder song in 1945
Could you believe in '54 Killer wouldn't be alive
Well he is gone to eternity
But his music and his words in my memory
He sang -
I am tired reading cases about murderers}
Everyday, everyday upon the newspapers} Repeat
Is either Sam kill Johnny or Johnny kill Joe
Is like a murder competition everywhere you go
We are in need of professional Scotland Yard
Detectives in Trinidad

*Photos of calypsonians mentioned may be projected. There are
no fixed items on stage as location throughout will be
created by the Chorus, which enters at the end of "Professor
Kitchener", with the "Young Brigade" theme song.*

Chorus: Young Brigade again
We young and we have the brain

Tell them we ain't 'fraid
We go mash up the Old Brigade

We come out to tease
A new bounce and beat if you please
Yes the time is right
Ladies, no more Old Brigade from tonight

It is an evening in, say, the late forties. The Chorus (three or four couples) wear the sleek, razor-sharp look of entertainers of the period. During their song, Ribero and helpers set up the place which Ribero has proudly dubbed 'Wonders Never'.

Figskin: (TIE-TONGUE MOPSY)
Last night I had a romance
with a tie tongue mopsy   } repeat
Who then confessed that she so love me}
She said Kitch I am all alone at home tonight
You can sleep because my grandmother
gone out of sight
I felt so glad that I lie down on the bed
But with a tie-tongue language the mopsy said.

Chorus: Lord Kitchener darling, get up
My grandmother coming twelve o'clock
Is twenty five to twelve get up
My grandmother coming twelve o'clock

Well friends you can imagine how I felt so badly
To know I had to leave her company
I spoke every English word that reach my memory
Just to apprehend her sympathy
I said dear, you know I will not dissemble
My love for you is inexpressible
And still with all I can try to break her heart
In the same tie-tongue language the mopsy start

Well then I made a promise to engage the mopsy
At the earliest opportunity
So she came around my shoulders
and started to hug me
As though she had some strange hilarity
Well in the midst of romance I simply stole a kiss
And then I request the little stupidness
She said "no twelve o'clock is coming near"
And in the same tie-tongue language she then
declared

Well friend when I saw she was so hard to persuade
I then consider I had to invade
So I held on to the craft with a determination
Regardless to all her objections
In a clinch I notice she start to bite and squeeze
I couldn't cope because I had a weakness in my knees
Then I hear a rapping, the grandmother call
Well with a louder volume the mopsy bawl

Chorus: Lord Kitchener darling, get up
My grandmother reach is twelve o'clock
Don't go through the front door get up
The ol' lady reach is twelve o'clock.

Ming: *(Has been making the round of the audience with his hat.
Shows figskin the proceeds.)*

Figskin: Aye, Ribero! You and this audience is family or
what? They so tight wind can't pass.

Ribero: You can blame them? Who want to hear a
calypsonian going by the sobriquet 'The Mighty
Figskin?' People waiting on Spoiler and the real
Kitchener.

Figskin: Me and Ming as good as Spoiler and Kitch!

Ribero: Hah!

Ming: In any case Spoiler dead to the world and Kitch ain't here.

Figskin: The problem ain't we name but the name of this place. Everybody know about 'Dirty Jim Swizzle' and 'Calypso Rendezvous' but 'Wonders Never'? What is a 'never'?

Ming: And if the never never have a wonder then why anybody must come to the never, ever?

Ribero: I have the cheapest drinks in town. You fellows either come up with new ideas or take a stroll. The name stays.

Figs: Ming, show this man how we could out-Kitch Kitchener heself. Ladies and gentlemen, presenting....

Ribero: The Lord Outhouse!

Ming: (MAN IN THE WARDROBE)
I am aware
That something is there so bring out the key
And open the wardrobe in front of me

Chorus: A man in the wardrobe Vio
Why the hell it shaking up so
A man in the wardrobe Vio
This two foot rat I would like to know

In front me eye
You telling a lie

But darling I know
Is more than a rat that shaking up so.

Chorus

The mister inside
You told him to hide
So open the door
Before ah buss a lash in he jaw

Chorus

You had it plan
To bring in a man
But you didn't know
That I would have come back and catch you so.

Chorus

You did it to me
In 1950
I'll never forget
When you hide a man in the cabinet.

*(Confronts a member of the Chorus 'Gaza' who responds
in role of the accused woman in the song. At end of song she
plants a kiss on Figskin - her 'man in the wardrobe'.)*

Ming: Well, I never!

Ribero: My wife do that!   I use my gun one time!

Gaza: With that half-dead gun you have where you could
find wife?

Ribero: My gun loaded and well-oiled, thank you.

Spoiler: *(From the bench where he was sleeping)*
That is joke. You ain't see nutten yet.

Ribero: At last he up.

Gaza: All the way, Ribero? Is a miracle!

Chorus: Take it away!

Ribero: Is Wonders Never!

Chorus: Sing it out, boys!

Spoiler: Lemme finish this fortifier.

Chorus: Ah wanna fall!

Spoiler: *(Downs remains of a drink)*
(ALL FOOLS DAY)
I thought I was cool   }
But is now I realise that I'm still a fool   } repeat
Believe I never realise this thing until
All Fool's Day on the 1st of April
Believe I would have kill my wife and the brute
If I feel she wasn't telling Spoiler the truth.

Chorus: I never see more belief in my life
Meet a man inside my own house kissing my wife
I ask what is that, she turn round and say
We only fooling you Spoiler, is All Fool's Day.

Ah ha, I bawl out oh-ho
Because I know that my wife never get on so
Partner, but my neighbour Lash
Use to tell me bout the man with the big moustache

I catch them kissing, I was telling Clarence
But is All Fool's Day I must leave allowance
Clarence watch me, pat me on the back
Tell me not to blame she, blame the almanac.

Chorus

Ah ha, what make the thing worse
The man inside my house he started to curse
Partner, Harold is he name
And he telling me my wife long time is he dame
She fool me again and she hug up Harold
You know the man kiss my wife on she eyeball
I bet you a house I tell Harold flat
On the 2nd of April you can't do that.

Chorus

Ah ha, some stupid husband
Would have start to make noise and
break they wife hand
Partner, they should take it cool
For on the first of April, you bound to get fool
So if you see your wife with Tom, Dick or Harry
On All Fool's Day, I beg you to leave she
Nothing you could do better in this world
Than to leave she alone let she rock and roll.

Ribero: Now that is kaiso!

Figs: *(To Spoiler)* You was out like a light. We had was to start the show.

Spoiler: All you make enough noise to wake up the dead. Shock me out of a good good dream. I dream I was..... I was .... Oh gorm, is gone the dream gone.

Gaza: Spoils, what you have for your doux-doux? You come like a dream come true.

Spoiler: A pocketful of kaiso. Things dry like bone. Ribero, trust the Spoils a lil gambi till I collect some camadeen.

Ming: 'Gambi'? 'Camadeen'?

Ribero: I ain't know what you say, nuh Spoiler, but I pick out the word 'trust' and you calypsonians know that is
one English word don't use in this establishment at all.

Ming: And that is the only English word the man use.

Gaza: 'Trust', Mr. Ribero, mean give we a drink now and charge we tomorrow for two. Is a technique your people invent.

Ming: Spoils, where you get that language from?

Spoiler: It call Spoilese and that is a story longer than the longest story ever told.

Figs: You could just put the drinks on the house. As a lil encouragement?

Ribero: Figs, you want Ribero to bust? Then you all self shift to 'The Black Cat' or that new Chinese place? Never happen. You boys bring in more people you get your share. Not before.

Figs: We bring in Gaza. You trying to say Gaza ain't people? That she ain't even worth a drink? True she had she days, but.....

Gaza: You damn fast! What I have is more than you so could pay for. War done and not much Yankees around but I still ain't want no damn calypsonian. Ribero, doods, I have a present for you, if you could manage.

Ribero: Can't afford it, Gaza. Too poor.

Gaza: You mean too old. You pay me for that baseball bat yet?

Ribero: On the spot. $3.50US. Your friends here witness it.

Figs: Gaza girl, you come like the War, over and done with. Like one of them batter-up ol' battleship the British leave back.

Gaza: Figs, you want to see a brand new war start in here tonight? When I done with you, ol' as you think I is, bet you, you end up lost in action'.

Spoiler: That's it! The song that did dream he way in my head. Hear this.

(FOUNTAIN OF YOUTH)
Suppose it happen in truth
Something spring up call the Fountain of Youth
If is on a mountain peak in the sky
People going for a bath don't care if they die
Imagine a man a hundred years old
See him how he climbing a greasy pole
You could be old like any King Kong
As you take a bath you coming back young

Chorus: See my great grandfather playing hop-scotch and pitching marble

And my great grandmother with a hula hoop
making trouble
The old people today in town
You could hear them talking bout
when they was young
But with the fountain they will be bold
The whole talk go change to when they was old.

Ol' people today who know that they old
Never had the chance to dance rock and roll
But with the fountain yes it will be hell
They will be supple like the snake they call macajuel
Those ol' women they go get the break
To put on their tight dress to walk and shake
All of them who canaree cover turn down
Hell on high water when they come back young

Chorus

Believe it or not I'll mention my name
The Spoiler, to tell you this I ain't shame
I done ol' me old as you all can see
And not a woman in the world ain't meddle with me
I heard that they say the Russians them soon
Decide to send men up in the moon
Well if is up there the fountain explode
Bet your life I'm the first man wha' want to go.

Chorus

See the Spoiler having women like he have chickens
I'll be young again so to me they will be some
easy pickings
I'll be walking about the place getting women with my
youthful face

I'll be flying like an aeroplane
Because I come back young I ain't old again.

Believe it or not I mean so to speak
You have to renew your bath once a week
Poor you, you ain't know you taking a stroll
With a woman about a hundred and three years old
She ain't renew the bath, you making your love
Talking 'bout the moon and the stars above
When you hear the shout say what you go do
She face turn like a salt prunes in front of you.

Chorus

You want to dead when you look at what
you was kissing
You cannot move cause your foot and them they ain't
even moving
And you trembling like a leaf
Can't get away from the young old beef
And she telling you kiss she, don't be afraid
Is forget she forget to renew she bathe.

Imelda: *(Enters during song)*
You don't have a care in this world, eh, Mr. Theophilus
Good-for-Nothing 'Phillip? Christmas could fall on
Good Friday. You don't have wife and children?

Ribero: And you wondering why I call here Wonder's Never'?
The customers questionable but the action is
guaranteed. Drinks anyone?

Imelda: Three whole weeks no money and is only dance you
dancing me with sweet talk.

Spoiler: Girl, this is a show, you know.

Imelda: Well, I too glad, cause I ready to show them your true colours.

Spoiler: Shh, shh! How much it is?

Imelda: Three weeks, Mr. Phillip, at $15 a week, the rate that the magistrate order you to pay.

Spoiler: Ribero....

Ribero: Sorry Spoils, even the patrons ain't buying tonight.

Spoiler: Imelda darling. you getting the money....

Imelda: I know, else is jail in your tail.

Spoiler: You know is off-season, so things ain't so pink....

Imelda: You win the Calypso Crown, not so? Where the money?

Spoiler: Look how long Carnival done! Besides the prize was two case of rum and I give that to charity.

Imelda: Well me ain't care! Season on or season off, my children have to eat. You is a big man. If you want to spend your life reading comic book and singing calypso in rumshop with these spongers that is your affair. I want my maintenance.

Figs: Spongers?

Spoiler: I will bring it give you at the end of this week.

Imelda: With your sleigh and reindeer? I will take it now please.

Spoiler: I brokes too bad girl.

Imelda: Too bad for you.

Chorus: *(To Young Brigade tune)*
When I tell you broke
I making no jest, I making no joke
Put the world in a pitch-oil tin
I can't even pay a cent to see the thing spin

Spoiler: Look! *(Turning pockets out)*

Imelda: You ain't have no shame, Theophilus, to be sitting down in a rum shop drinking day in day out and you can't mind your family? Is as plain as that. Is free rum this Portagee giving away? Since is a show, as you say, I will M.C.! *(To Figs)* You, move! Allyou! This man here, Theophilus, have three children with   me, he wife, that he can't mind. Last time I had was to take him before the magistrate to get my money. Before me, he had a child with a woman from Behind the Bridge. The child turn big man and join iron band. If he ain't see mine in weeks, he ain't see that boy in years. Next....

Spoiler: Well, leave something to the imagination, nuh?

Imelda: I telling them all. Next, he fraid courthouse for so, but if he can't come up with the goodies, crapaud smoke he pipe. Remember what happen last Christmas? Now, Mr. Theophilus put that in your calypso and sing it! *(Exits)*

Spoiler: Imagine the woman want to tell me what to sing
           and all?

Ribero: *(Handing him a drink)* On the house. This one is an
           emergency.

Figs: So am..... What really happen last Christmas?

Spoiler: A tale and a half.

           (FATHER CHRISTMAS)
           Since I small, I always believe   }
           Father Christmas does come on Christmas Eve} repeat
           When I small, I use to hang up my stockings
           So much of toys I use to get Christmas morning
           Now I big like a man-of-war
           Last year I hang up a rice bag in front my door.

           Chorus:
           Christmas morning I wake up early
           To see what Father Christmas bring for me
           He bring a police in a short pants (like Jack Palance)
           With a warrant for me for wife maintenance.

           You can bet the Federal Flag
           Greediness make me hang up the rice bag
           Why you think I do that because
           I thought I would have a thing on Santa Claus
           That when he passing with he reindeer
           As he spot my rice bag, he'll declare
           Spoiler is hungry,
           Let we put a couple roast pig in there for he

           Chorus

I never see more in my life
How the man know that I doesn't mind my wife
Right away I start to study
I decided, oh yes to make enquiry
I tie the police in the kitchen
I run down the road and I asking, I asking
I started to shake
When I hear Mother New Year give him the rake

Chorus

Christmas could be ten times a year
Not me again to hang nothing anywhere
Fuss I afraid of this Santa Claus
Next time he might put in a couple gunslingers
So when people making preparations
Spoiler will come to one conclusion
Let my house stop so
I wouldn't hang up a balloon in front my door

Ming: Best we pass the hat
again, for Spoiler this time.

Spoiler: I ain't want no charity. In fact I ain't want no
kind of tea. But if a drink is proffered.......

Gaza: The woman right.
Allyou man too damn watless.

Figs: Better yet, a fete. We could throw a dance this
Saturday and get more people in the club than
'Swizzle' or 'Rendezvous'. Ribero, you say you want
a new idea?

Ribero: What so new in a dance?

Figs: This is Spoiler's dance, a fete to turn age to youth and....

Ming: Youth to age?

Ribero: Jeezanages! Now he talking obeah!

Figs: The young will remain young forever!

Ming: A fountain of youth!

Figs: Figskin, you is a genius! Eh, Spoils? Ribero, how it sound?

Ribero: Very fine. But how am I and my club involved in your hoax?

Figs: Hoax? Ribero, Ribero, this is Trinidad, Carnival Country! Anything could happen! You have no sense of metaphor or what?

Gaza: Is the first sensible thing you say all night. But we must have a proper band, not no pick-up side. See your girl dancing the 'marico'.

Figs: I sure we could line-up Kitch, Preddie, Killer, Wonder...

Ribero: I wonder who paying for this big bram?

Ming: Money, money, money is all on Ribero mind.

Figs: See it this way, you putting out next to nothing for some hand bills, the cover charge paying band and singers and you selling liquor galore. How you could lose?

Ming: Spoils, what you say?

Spoiler: Saturday is three, four bottles away, friend. I will cruise down Frederick Road by Kitch and see if I could hustle some coinage.

Chorus: Take it away, Spoils!

Gaza: Ship in dock tomorrow. Tourists for so. You could try my luck.

Chorus: Ah wanna fall!

Spoiler: Well fall, nuh. *(Exits)*

Figs: Tourists? Ming what you say?

Scene II

Chorus: *(Young Brigade)*
Pick up the tempo
As we say, boys on with the show
For the road there is one Master
The man from Arima, Lord Kitchener.

Kitch: (OLD LADY WALK)
Waye aye aye, waye aye aye, and she tay lay lay
Waye aye aye, waye aye aye and she tay lay lay
Old lady walk a mile and a half
And she tay lay lay
Old lady walk a mile and a half
And she tay lay lay

Up the hill down the hill was Miss Betaudier
She was walking the distance to Point Fortin

Old lady walk a mile and a half and she tay lay lay
Old lady walk a mile and a half and she tay lay lay

She left home from Arima at 6:30
When she reach to Arouca she bazodee
Old lady walk a mile and a half and she tay lay lay
Old lady walk a mile and a half and she tay lay lay

With a Martiniquan towel she tied her head
In a basket she had two cassava bread
Old lady walk a mile and a half and she tay lay lay
Old lady walk a mile and a half and she tay lay lay

(They make room for entry of Ma Popo. She dances with grip on head, shoes lace-tied around her neck and a bag of ground provision in hand. A boy precedes her, pointing the way to Tina's door)

Popo: *(Knocking)* Tina! *(Gives boy a coin which he accepts with marked disappointment)*
Here. And thanks. What more you waiting on? *(Boy leaves sulkily)* Everything in this Port-of-Spain is the almighty dollar. Tina! Come chile, open this door. I walk too far for one door to stop me now.

Tina: Don't break it down, I coming. *(Opens)* What....Ma Popo? Is you? I don't believe my eyes.

Popo: Stand up there looking dotish before you look to ease up my load.

Tina: Sorry, come inside. You give me one shock, I thought was a ghost I seeing.

Popo: Lil more again and is that self. I almost dead reaching this Port-of-Spain.

Tina: But how you reach here in truth? How you find me? Gan-gan is so good to see you. *(Hugs)*

Popo: I was wondering if you wasn't going to greet your great grand aunt. I walk, nuh.

Tina: From Toco?

Popo: Take me three days, but I can't abide the motor vehicles and their crazy driving. Your father send this give you. *(Provision)* I could see you need some good food.

Tina: Pa well? And all them scamps at home?

Popo: Good as ever. How you and the madame going?

Tina: One day up one day down. But Pa, everybody alright?

Popo: I tell you they good. I leave them preparing for the funeral.

Tina: Lord in heaven! I just know was some bad news. Who dead?

Popo: Done the braying, chile. Nobody ain't dead.

Tina: But you say they having a funeral.

Popo: I say 'preparing'. It ain't happen yet, so don't start no wailing.

Tina: But who, Ma Popo? Who dying?

Popo: Chile, me. I going and dead.

Tina: You? But you strong as an ox, Gan-gan. You just
             walk from Toco.

Popo: Strength have nothing to do with it. My number call.

Tina: You sure? You see a doctor?

Popo: Doctor? I never went to one in my life, them and
             priests, and I not going by none to dead. The old
             people singing in my head nights in a row, that is how
             I know.

Tina: Oh, Gan-gan.

Popo: Oh, Gan-gan what? I live my life these years as I
             want it and I almost done with that. One thing, I
             ain't see Port-of-Spain. So I tell myself, Bernice, why
             you don't spend a few dollars and see the city before
             they pitch you in the gravel? After all,

             (DEATH IS COMPULSORY)
             Up to now I haven't seen the sense
             Why we should be grasping at opulence } repeat
             You can have money in quantity
             Like England, Japan and Germany
             Death is compulsory
             Six feet of earth and you gone to eternity.

Tina: Well, now I more glad to see you. Imagine
             I wouldn't even did know til....

Popo: Girl, cut the wailing. I don't have time to waste.
             I ready for Port-of-Spain.

Tina: Is not like Toco, you know, Gan-gan.

Popo: If it was I woulda stay home.

Tina: I mean the place pack up with scamp and ol' thief.
You can't trust nobody, police, lawyers, don't talk
about them taxi-drivers!

Popo: I hear all that already. I ready to go.

Tina: Well, it have the Princes Building, the Colonial
Hospital and them big-shot houses round the
Savannah. Which you want to see first?

Popo: They was handing out these
pamphlets in town.

Tina: *(Reads)* All Night Dance? At the Fountain of Youth?

Chorus: For the young at heart
Action is guaranteed from the start
Come and dance the marico
And hear the best singers of Calypso.

Popo: We going deck off in the latest fashion. Port of
Spain, ready or not Ma Popo reach!

Scene III

*(A street in Port-of-Spain. Calypsonians, taxi-drivers,
vendors of one sort or another tackle a group of tourists)*

Figs: (NYLON MAN, NYLON WOMAN)
My grandmother use to wear flour bag
But now these modern girls they walk about and brag

My mother in law and my girlfriend Anne
When they dress they does look so transparent
But if I didn't have control, believe me
I would have invade the whole family

They wearing nylon dress, nylon dress
Nylon nightie and you know the rest
Nylon man, ah hah
Nylon woman, ah hah
Nylon this, ah hah
Nylon that, ah hah
Yes, they walking the street naked as they born
Selling they property to buy nylon

I went to a dance with one Eva Thorne
Everything she had on was nylon
Nylon eyelash and nylon hair net
Nylon lipstick that I can't forget
Nylon suit and nylon stocking
She was looking so fascinating
She had on a nylon brassiere and all
She attracted everybody in the dance hall

Tourist 1: *(Applauds)* Great! That some kind of folk song?

Figs: Calypso. We native song.

Tourist 2: Calypso? The agent told us Jamaica was the land of Calypso and this here's the land of...

Kitch: The Steelband?

Tourist 1: Naw, the hibiscus, he said.

Tourist 2: Yeah, and Tobago the land of the Humming Bird. Or was it the other way around?

Tourist 3:   Who cares? Hey, can you guys do a real Harry
Belafonte calypso? I mean, like the genuine thing?

Kitch: Harry who? Listen mister, Calypso come from right
here in Trinidad. We make it and we make the
Steelband too. Hear this.

(BEAT OF THE STEELBAND)
Well I heard the beat of the steelband
Boys I couldn't understand
It was hard to make a distinction
Between Poland, Bar Twenty and John John.

Chorus:
Pung Pang ba duba do bang}
Pung Pang ba duba do bang}Repeat

Port of Spain nearly catch afire
When the band was crossing the Dry River
Zigelee leader of the Ping Pong
Had people jumping wild in the town.

Black James, Fish Eye and Barker
Bar Twenty leading kittle-beater
I jump until I couldn't jump again
Was sweeter than George Smith from Edwin Payne.

Bitter-Man, Pops and Battersby
Chop in with a semitone melody
When they start their contrary beat
White people jumping wild in the street.

Well the boom was beaten by Ossey
A foreman boomer from Bar Twenty
The vibration near break down a wall
An American say, "Joe don't stop at all".

Chamberlain had me going crazy
I thought we was still fighting Germany
When the man blow the bugle call
I said "Well, like the war ain't finish at all!"

(During which Gaza and a taxi-driver enter)

Tourist 1:   That's fabulous!

Spoiler: The hat is for any lil appreciation.

Gaza: How about it, honey? To heaven and back?

Tourist 3:   What's the cost of the trip?

Driver: Stop pestering the people, woman! Is broad daylight!
You ain't fraid? Go find your hole! Taxi at your
service, sir. You all see Maracas yet? The Pitch Lake?
Tobago?

Gaza: (TAXI-DRIVERS) *(She is joined
by calypsonians who extemporise to the delight of the tourists)*

The taxi-drivers of this city
To the pedestrians is a real worry } repeat
You can be standing on any pavement
Answer more questions than than the government
All you see is taxis in a line
And all you do is answering questions all the time.

Chorus:

For is 'Beep! One to go!
You shake your head, you tell him no
Blah! They blow in vain
You shake you head, you tell them no again.

(Spoken) And is San Juan, Tunapuna, Arima,
Sangre Grande
Movement with love. Madam you going?
I'm the fella who give you a lift in
Toco last week, you can't remember me?
And they pointing their finger all over the place
Somebody have a right to spit in their face.

When these taxi-drivers ain't got a conscience
In long and in short, they are a perfect nuisance
They break every rule and every regulation
Don't talk about the charge they
calling obstruction
They have a way of rocking inside a canal
Blocking traffic from
Queen Street to the Hospital
And if a policeman just make an attack
Well they
hand him two bob and they done with that.

Spoiler: Don't neglect the hat..

Constab 1:   *(Entering)* Eh-heh, I catch all you this time. Soliciting
on a public street. Gimme that hat. Is evidence.

Figs: Soliciting? So what about he, the taxi-driver?

Constab 1:   Taxi is a licensed trade. They entitle to ply the
streets.

Driver: Take them down, Constable. They thief a whole
day's work. And the woman too.

Kitch: I know that police face....

Spoiler: Ever see 'Fallen Angels' with Jack Palance?

Figs: Them licensed and we is what? What is calypsonian in this Trinidad?

Tourist 2: See, the agent was right. Sure it's Jamaica that's the land of the calypso.

Constab 1: Tomorrow you could ask the magistrate. One more question and I slap on the charge they call obstructing the law.

Tourist 1: Hey, you guys were great. Sorry you got into this spot.

Constab 1: Now, all, down the road!

Imelda: *(Enters with another constable)*
There he is, Officer. That's my husband!

Constab 2: You there! You under arrest!

Spoiler: Again? Well I never see nothing so.

Constab 1: Take a rest. He arrest already. I taking him in!

Constab 2: You doing what? This lady bring she complaint to me. Is my charge.

Constab 1: Charge him if you want, but I is taking him in. I arrest him.

Constab 2: I on this case. He going in with me.

Constab 1: Aye mister, who arrest you first, not me?

Spoiler: All I know, this have the makings of a first class kaiso.

Constab 2: What is he name? You don't even know and you making arrest. What you charge him with?

Constab 1: Both a we is the same rank, since when I must answer to you? And who say you have to know name to make an arrest? Where you learn this work? In Grenada?

Constab 2: What you bringing Grenada in this for? You want me tell the public why you get transfer fromCumuto?

Constab 1: You dog! Is slander you come to slander my name? Take this!

Constab 2: Nah, I ain't taking that. Lady, hold me charge book. First you thiefing cow, now you thiefing prisoner?

Kitch: Tell you I know that face! Is Constable Joe, the cow thief from Cumuto!

(CONSTABLE JOE)
If you miss the scandal, you get it now
Constable Joe caught stealing a cow

Chorus:
Constable Joe we know
You thief the cow in Cumuto

Constable Joe was crafty and bright
He painted the heifer in black and white
Constable Joe had nothing to say
When the magistrate said "Take him away"

Chorus

Say what you like it is my belief
That every policeman is a thief

Gaza: Heave!

Driver: Heave!

(As policemen wade into each other, Calypsonians make good their escape)

Scene IV

Kitch: Chinese Clipper Restaurant!

Spoiler: What we doing here? Ain't Chin say he
              ain't want no calypso in he place?

Figs: Give me Tantie Tea Shop any day.

Kitch: How much we could collect at Tantie Tea Shop?
              Any case I have Tantie, teashop and all already
              under wraps. We will sweet talk Chin. Let we get
              them customers smiling.

Figs: Paying.

Kitch: (V. J. DAY)
              Try and remember the tenth of October
              Just try and remember, the tenth of October
              Some kind of Chinese memorial
              Ended in real Monday Carnival
              Town people get hot brain
              When the Chinee people near burn down
              Port of Spain.

Chorus:
Lay oh pongtang ee aye,
Lai fook lee ah lowsee aye
Lay oh pongtang ee aye,
Chinee never had a VJ Day
Lay oh pongtang ee aye,
Lai fook lee ah low see aye

Sleeping in me cacheau,
In my dream I hearing a echo
Poor Kitchener sleepy,
But the Chinee have me bazodee
I jump out my bed when I feel the heat
I bounce up a band now crossing George Street
I nearly dead with laugh
I find myself in the arm of a Chinese craft.

Chorus

This I bound to mention,
A joke with a Chinee lion
Big men frighten like fire,
Thinking is a true lion come from China
Just by a mistake the lion groan
John drop he base on a saxophone
People get misled
Was a Chinee playing mas in a lion head.

Chorus

This was disagreeable
I can't understand we people
The boys cry out they hungry
The Chinese decide to take us at Chin Lee
As soon as the waitress bring the dish

Big-eye Agnes thief a slice of fish
I didn't forget to hide
They make every black Chinee go outside.

Chin: *(Enters)* No, no, no! No singing in restaurant at all!

Kitch: Whappen, Chin? You mightn't like calypso, but you in Trinidad. Look how the customers happy.

Figs: It go help them digest some of that rancid pork you does cook.

Chin: He bad mouth my food, I sue he chop, chop! Chin no fool.

Kitch: You surprise me man, Chin. You is the only Chinee I know ain't like a lil bacchanal. You letting down your side.

Chin: Alright, alright, sing two, three nice song while Chin finish food, but no pester customers or else!

Figs: Don't worry, Chin, we does live on wind.
(Chin exits to kitchen)

Chorus: Today for the special
Chin serving 'Kaiso Bacchanal'
You could get a whole plate free
If you come out and sing a chorus with we.

(Individual members of audience invited to come up and sing a chorus of any favorite song).

Ming: *(Entering)* How all you could come in a Chinese restaurant and leave out the Mighty Ming Foo?

(CHINESE CRICKET MATCH)
I had a read on yesterday's papers
A cricket match with some Chinese players (repeat)
They say the Indian people name funny
Nothing to beat the Chinee
As though the Chinese does get their name
By the beating of the steelband in Port of Spain.

Chorus:
For is Ling King
Bowled and caught by Loong Ping
And Wing Ping
Got cleaned bowled by Poon Pang
And the whole Oval shout
When Loom Lum get Wang Poon Ping Pang Poon out.

I was in a lacouray
I reading 'bout the thing yesterday
I bit my tongue on several occasions
To make the right pronunciation
You must be graduated in China
To pronounce these Chinese names proper
'Cause, as I understand
They get their names to the sounding of a tin pan.

Chorus

Wing Ping Sing one of the umpires
He made a sign to the scorers
He said,'ling ling ling pang ping loom long
That meant that they made a short run
The Chins started a fighting
Saying the umpire was stealing
And friends, you could believe me
When I finish read, I was talking Chinee.

Spoiler: (WENT TO COLLEGE)
I had the privilege
Last year to buy books and go to college,
The Spoiler had the privilege,
Last year to buy books and to go to college
But when it come to subjects like grammar,
Mathematics and thing so they couldn't beat Spoiler
But anytime I spell people say I mad
But I am the best speller come from Trinidad

Hear my spelling
K-A-P-P-O-L-A-I-N aeroplane,
M-A-P-P-O-S-P-A-N-E Port of Spain
A-N-E-Y-P-A-L that's Carnival,
A-G-T-Y-B-R-A-L is Cathedral

It comes to subjects like Spanish
I know more of that than I know the English
I know si is yes, papel is paper
Madre is mother, padre is father
Beside that I use to collect my money well
For fun the pupils use to pay me to spell
And the teachers use to give me back my school fee
They thought me too bright to take my money

Because I spelling
K-A-P-P-O-L-A-I-N aeroplane
M-A-P-P-O-S-P-A-N-E Port of Spain
E-N-N-E-Y-M-E-E enemy
J-O-G-G-R-A-F-E-E geography

It came to examination
They decided to ask me a couple questions
The first question was what is grammar?
I told them the wife of my old grandfather
The second question was what is a clause?

I told them the nails on the pussy paws
Well the teacher told me I should be in hell
But I ain't business with he, I know I could spell.

Hear my spelling
K-A-P-P-O-L-A-I-N   aeroplane
M-A-P-P-O-S-P-A-N-E Port of Spain
K-A-N-D-L-E-S-T-Y-K candlestick
K-R-I-K-K-M-A-T-I-K arithmetic

It came down to the vacation
They decided to have some prize distribution
Tommy got special prize for Algebra
Cornelius got special prize for Literature
They hand me my prize, it was neatly wrapped
You can imagine how I felt everybody clapped
But when I open the prize what you think in it
A dunce cap and a revolver with one bullet.

Because I spelling
K-A-P-P-O-L-A-I-N   aeroplane
M-A-P-P-O-S-P-A-N-E Port of Spain
E-N-N-E-Y-M-E-E enemy
J-O-G-G-R-A-F-E-E geography

Figs: (HINDU WEDDING)
This is really true,   }
I decide this year to marry a Hindu} Repeat
So is hundreds of Indians gather
Yes in my teloke in Marabella, aha
Man Pooran get crazy
When they start with the sweet melody

Chorus:
Singing jago jago sheylam, jago jago sheylam
Ot ki ki dingah da dam ki ka dam

Things now getting sweet,
And fling a set a dhal back for me to eat
Lord, is pepper like fire
I can't stand the burning I bawling for water
So big-belly Ramlal, come
With a coolie drum and a dhantal

Chorus

Singing every time I passing gal
you grinding massala } Repeat
Grinding massala, grinding massala
And every time I passing well she grinding massala

I can't get a chance,
Ramsingh scrambled me we started to dance
Lord, Ruth, Soojan and Boodie
The three maharajh in the ceremony
So Facil and Pharaoh
They drink they grog, they start with they leggo

Chorus

Singing bombay say doolahini di
array dabouji }Repeat

So these few apaches,
Took part in the ceremony
Well yes is Apang, Bachan, Ahir,
Goondir, Ramdan and Sookhir
Lord, I had to laugh at Palchan
These guys playing American

Chorus

Singing tousan Amelican landed in Port of Spain
Some come by battle ship, some come by yaeroplane

(During this last song, Imelda re-enters with Constable 2, his arm in a sling)

Imelda: Theophilus, today is me, you and this arm of the law! Arrest him, Mr. Constable! *(Calypsonians dodge around tables, etc)*

Chin: *(enters with chopper)*
You come to mash up Chin place?
I make creole soup with your tail!
(Charges with chopper. All exit rapidly.)

Chorus: Chin ain't eating nice.
Nobody, he say, not fooling he twice
He put up a sign in front the crowd
'No Dogs and Calypsonians Allowed'.

Scene V

(Ma Popo and Tina with shopping bags pause before a roadside preacher, Sales)

Sales: And Death, it says here, dear sisters shall have no dominion. But what is the price, (since as we know nothing is free) of life eternal? How do we, dying creatures all, defy and defeat this final fact of our mortal flesh? The answer is right here, my dear ones: Shed ye the things of this world.' In other words calculate, calculate! *(To Ma Popo)* How can you reach the summit of eternal life Miss Lady, laden like the rich man's ass with the weight of the world? *(To Tina)* So my child, lay them down, your worries, your woes, your bags, your body and any small change you might happen to have, right here so together we can journey to that summit!

Tina :   (FOLLOW ME CHILDREN)
They got a lot of preachers that is preaching round
the town
If I was a police well I was sure to take
some down   } repeat
Ah for the man that say he's Christ
Mama well he always dress up nice
So much a pretty gown
Don't talk about his golden crown
Fooling people in town.

Chorus:
Follow me children you will never die
Wai yai yai look water in me eye
Follow me children you will never die
Remember Noah in the Ark
And you bound to do your part
Follow me children you will never die

Those scamps wouldn't shave they moustache
or they beard
They wouldn't trim they hair well if you see those
people head
And fuss I love to hear those monsters croon
They really got some sweet calypso tune
Then the garment very nice
For Carnival they sure to get first prize
They got the song and they got the pretty gown
Is trouble in town.

One night I take me fastness and I went up
Hill and Hall
When I reach the door they wouldn't let me pass at all
I had to use the password which is peace be unto you.
A fellar with a sword then let me through

Yes I did fraid the mallet man
He pose off like the Killer in the band
A woman with a big glass of water in she hand
Wetting down the smart man

(They exit toward end of song as Calypsonians enter)

Sales: Where you going, brother ? You missing the chance
of a lifetime, the ascent of the soul to Mt. Zion!

Figs: Not the ascent is the scent, when last water touch
your skin?

Sales: I baptise just before the War, brother, and look what
happen. You want a next war start again? All you
looking desperate. I is Doctor Sales, erstwhile
psychiatrist, retired jurist, ex-poet, bespoke inventor,
practising preacher, a salesman of salvation,
so to speak.

Figs: Bespoke inventor?

Sales: And bicycle mechanic. It have problems ain't invent
yet that I could fix.

Spoiler: What about problems that around a long time?
Like yourself?

Sales: Alas, brother, I mad like hell.

Kitch: You could make a man who wife looking for
him vanish?

Sales: Vanish? Hmm....nah, not varnish but I have some
black paint...

Spoiler: All you ain't hear the damn man
mad? Not me and no bespoke inventor, nuh.

(WORLD OF TOMORROW)
A scientist fella he made me to know   } Repeat
What happen in the world of tomorrow }

I can get up anytime in the afternoon
Imelda darling, let's go to the moon
She'll say, Spoiler darling you're making fun
We went to moon last week let's go to the sun

Chorus:
The scientist say so help me blest
People will make children by wireless
If you live for those days you'll be shocked to see
Monkey joining like man in matrimony

He was telling me about a nine legged duck
Suddenly at my front door I heard a knock
I thought it was my daughter or my girl friend
But to my great surprise was four policemen
They arrest the scientist I said look men
This scientist fellar in here is my friend
The police say scientist? Spoiler not this louse
He's a mad man that run way from the mad house.

The scientist say so help me blest
People will get children by wireless
You quite up the road, your wife here alone
And all you could make children on the telephone.

Sales: *(Interrupts song as he seems to be listening to a sound in the
atmosphere only he can hear)*
Wait, wait! I hearing it! You catch it? *(Starts to wine,
mumble)*

Figs: The man like he talking in tongues!

Spoiler: And wining so? Look, let we speed, yes.

Sales: (*Blurts out*) Calypso of tomorrow!

               (SUGAR BUMBUM)
               Audrey where you get that sugar
               Darling there is nothing sweeter
               You make me squeal, you make me bawl
               You make me feel like ten feet tall
               Sugar bum, sugar bum bum
               Sugar bum, sugar bum bum

Kitch: That you calling calypso? Where the lyrics?

Sales: Not me, people of tomorrow.

Spoiler: Come tomorrow story in calypso dead and bury?
               You ain't just mad, you mental!

Kitch: If I was to take you serious I stop singing calypso
               one time.

Sales: Listen for allyou self. (*They try*)

Imelda: (*Enters with a limping Constable 2*)
               There! And don't let him get away this time.

Constab: Lady, I know my job.

Imelda: You able, nuh?

Figs: I ain't hear a damn thing.

Spoiler: I tell all you if that man say stand still, run.

Imelda: *(Ahead of the hobbling Constable)*
            Look, gimme that warrant!

Sales: *(Spotting Constable)* Run!

Spoiler: You see what I mean? Bluff.

Imelda: *(Grabbing Spoiler)* Now, Mr. Theophilus, is arrest you
            under.

Constab   Madam! Lady! Miss! Take it easy, please!
            (Others run off)

Imelda: *(To Constable)* You ain't arresting him? All you
            man does stand up for one another.

Spoiler: The woman turn woman police now.

Imelda: And that is what you did want?

            (WOMAN POLICE)
            They should have woman police in Trinidad }
            Bet your life Spoiler would be more than glad } Repeat
            I only waiting till one keeping duty
            I running right away and I kissing she
            And when she snatch on to me I wouldn't say a word
            But I hugging up my police going down the road

            Chorus
            (And all the time) I pulling
            away from she for she to hold me tight
            The woman police must hold me tight
            And I doing all that for spite
            For she to hold me tight, tight, tight

            A feller told me they would be more bad
            Than the male police we have in Trinidad

But I don't care, they can be hard like a cobra
Don't talk when you see I drink my liquors
And I butting from west to east
I walking right away and hug up my police
She can hold me round me neck And squeeze me
till I dead
But I kissing from she waist right up to she head

Chorus

And when she carry me inside the charge room
I coupling up me police like a bridegroom
When the female sergeant ask me anything
Is a heap of doodoo darling I answering
Honey chooks my love please forget
I know by the way she would start to fret
But she can beat me, she can butt me Tear down
my clothes
I ain't retreating, I advancing for my blows

Constab: Down to the station, Mr. Phillip!

Spoiler: But you ain't even hear my side.

Constab: That, Mr. Phillip, is for the magistrate.

Spoiler: But you holding the wrong man!

Constab: I see enough trouble to issue this warrant. You
deny you is Mr. Phillip, the husband of this woman?

Imelda: Don't try no tricks. I have you in a tip-toe grip.

Spoiler: Yes and no. You arresting the wrong Mr. Phillip.

Imelda: This one I have to hear.

Spoiler: (TWIN BROTHER)
Have you heard, yes, about my twin brother}
Was the spitting image of Spoiler   } Repeat
Both of we, we had the same face
Same kind of hair, the same size of waist
The same every thing you ask Mr. Wilk
Like two tin of the same make of condense milk

Chorus:
If he playing football, I in the stand
I sit down with my woman name Lillian
And if he miss a ball, she will turn around
Telling me I's the worst footballer in town

From the time Spoiler and his brother born
Believe I was the bad luck one Oh Lord
We reach the age of sixteen he get married
Leave his wife and he had to speed
I didn't mind that didn't worry me
I too went and join in matrimony
Well the day of my wedding, up came his wife
And she make one of the biggest mistake in life

She walk in the church with Constable Dan
Pointing at the Spoiler, 'That's my husband'
My twin brother she take he for me
And they hold me and charge me for bigamy.

Constab: You and your wife who is not your wife have my
head feeling like it ain't my head. I shoulda really left
you with that cow thief of a police in the first place.
Let we go. *(Exit with Spoiler and wife)*

Scene VI

Kitch: *(Alone)* (MY WIFE GONE)
My wife left me in November
To go with a yankee soldier} Repeat
She said Kitch I am so sorry
But you can't afford to make me happy
I told her darling come back to me
She shook her head so pitifully

Chorus: Kitch don't look so sad
I may join you back in Trinidad
I have made up my mind to go
You can't support me on calypso

I turned and said to my darling
Why it is you are leaving
She said you might not believe me
But the yankee has plenty money
And since I have him as my boyfriend
I get a lot of money to spend
So Kitchie darling you must agree
That is what you can't give to me

I said dear you should know better
Than to fall in love with a soldier
A man who lives like a hermit
And hires himself as a target
She says your criticism is fine
But you cannot make me change my mind
I don't care what you think of me
Tomorrow I bound for New York City

(At Wonders Never)
Ribero: But this is real trouble. Band in place, everything set.
People coming to this fete to hear Spoiler and

	Kitchener. And you telling me Spoiler down at the station and Kitch have what?

Figs: Domestic problems. Went to his wife bedroom without knocking.

Ribero: So what I must do? Tell the people they have to wait till Kitch and he wife kiss and make back? I know this was a hoax from the start.

Figs: Leave everything in the hands of the Lord Figskin and me partner here. Me and Ming done map out we strategy already, who singing what, eh, Ming?

Ming: Like we have some early birds.

Ribero: Whole show in hands of Lord Figskin and the Mighty Ming Foo! I might as well be running a Chinese Restaurant!
(Returns to bar as Tina and Ma Popo enter dressed to kill. Low whistles from band)

Figs: Well, tonight must be the glory night. Ladies, let me welcome you to the Fountain of Youth! The best spot in town. Tonight is fete galore.

Popo: Wha' kinda fete is this? The place dead.

Figs: Well you ladies reach first, but I sure that with your looks all the boys will be traipsing in right behind.

Tina: I wonder what on down at the Rendezvous?

Figs: Care for some drinks? Bartender! Service!

Ribero: *(Glares, but complies)*

Popo: I hear is calypso action here tonight.

Figs: All night. See the band ready? Best band in town.

Tina: And these big names, they on the programme?

Figs: Every single one.

Tina: Oh hoh! Is my first visit and I ain't want to get disappoint.

Figs: First time in a club? You too?

Popo: You know how it is with old fashioned parents, nuh. Is only now we come of age.

Figs: Well, you ladies real lucky tonight. This is your chance to meet the big guns.

Tina: Any of them here?

Figs: Look, Lord Kitchener there *(Ming)*

Tina: The doorman?

Figs: He just holding on. This is a benefit for we pardner Spoiler, nuh, so we don't want any extra expense. I can't keep calling you 'you ladies' whole night.

Tina: I is Tina and this is....

Popo: Bernice. We is sisters. *(To Tina)* You ain't find the bartender cute?

Figs: Ribero? Well they say the place is Wonders Never. Bernice, Tina, the stars at your command tonight, me, Kitch.

Tina: And you is who?

Figs: You don't have to "wonder. "

(UGLY AS SIN)
Chorus:
For when they reasoning high
You dig out me eye
And when your reasoning low
No no no
A woman ugly as sin I would love her
With good reasoning.

Figs: This calypso season   }
I want a keeper with plenty reason   } Repeat
No matter how you pretty and fat
You can't trap me if you ain't carrying that
A woman without reason should really dead
She like a crapaud without neck but carrying a head.

Yes I went in at Salvatori
A girl was buying a blue dress next to me
When she call for five yards and a half
You know the clerk just buss out a big laugh
I said Miss this dress is for you ?
She said yes sir and it mightn't do
Is when the young lady was leaving the store
I see the reason she shoulda buy more.

Yes reason have Tina bawling
She can't walk in peace someone always calling
"Doey, dear, hello"
When she got on this tight wear
Cyclists running into cars
Scientist peeping down from Mars

Aeroplane crashing into trees
This time I praying for she to reason with me.

(More people enter dance)

Band: *(Plays a charleston as couples including Figs
and Tina, Ming and Ma Popo dance the marico)*

Figs: Ladies and gentlemen, tonight's fete is a benefit for
our good friend and reigning Calypso King, the
Mighty Spoiler. But none of this woulda happen
without the help of the owner of The Fountain of
Youth', Mr. Ribero. A round of applause, please!
Ribero, take a bow.

Ribero: *(Comes forward)* Friends, I happy to help the
calypsonians. Just keep buying drinks, and I will
keep helping. Now, is years these fellas in my bar
and I listening to them sing and is just so I start
making up a little tune here, a few words there until
I come up with something I want to try tonight.

Figs: Tonight, Ribero?

Ribero: Now! Is a special song from a secret admirer. *(Winks
at Ma Popo)* My calypso name is 'Pharaoh'. Allyou
like how it sound? Lemme hear it.

Crowd: Pharaoh!

Ribero: (PORTUGUESE DANCE)
Chorus:
Visk ke visk ke vo
Visk ke visk ke vi
Visk ke visk ke vo
Ve vi vo vi...

The Pharaoh jump in a Portagee dance
While the music is playing
If you see how Portagee he jumping Lord
I jump for a part
For the very number to break down my heart

I mean the both of them on the programme
Every Portagee buy a ten round
One pick up a guitar
To play a Portagee rhumba
While the people dancing
If you see how Portagee grinning, lord
I dip for a part
For the very number to break down my heart

Sometimes he throw too much flour
Well I thief a Portagee mooma
Tell me King Pharaoh I love you
Please what I going to do, lord
So do understand Pharaoh
I want to romance
Man please have a care
The girl want to touch me with a goose flare
(Lights go down on all dancing to Pharoah's roadmarch)

Act 2

Scene I

Spoiler: *(Alone in the charge room, muses)*
(TALKING BACKWARD)
Suppose every woman could have afford   }
To sit down and learn how to talk backward} Repeat

Instead of saying oh me backward is me oh
Instead of saying oh dear backward is dear oh
And when they talk so we poor men wouldn't understand
So all the woman will have advantage on man

And if a woman want to leave she man
She go talk it he can't understand
She wouldn't say Maryann I will leave the man
She'll just say man the leave will I Maryann

The women will be tinging we up for so
They will be bad talking we and we wouldn't know
They wouldn't say that fellar face like an alpagat
They will say alpagat an like face fellar that
And believe me friends where we go get the blow
Is if they start to do the housework backward also
I sure plenty husbands go run and hide
Cattle sleeping inside man sleeping outside

And if a woman want to leave she man
She go talk it he can't understand
She wouldn't say Ruby I will leave Johnny
She'll just bawl out Johnny leave will I Ruby

Well with this backward business they getting through
They will start to do everything backward too
Instead of throwing the water in the flour
They go start to throw the flour in the water
And when you see this thing get chronic in their blood
They will forget entirely how to talk forward
Husband can't understand wife what she saying
Wife can't understand husband well that is thing

And when she ask him for the allowance
Well the husband will be in a monkey pants

She wouldn't say Johnny where is my money
She'll just bawl out money my is where Johnny

Then she will put him in front of the magistrate
And all she worries she'll try to relate
The magistrate too will be in a monkey pants
Because he wouldn't understand the sentence
Then he go jump off he bench and bawl
Woman I cannot understand you at all
I tell you to come straight outside my place
Go and see if you get a devil to try your case

(During song, transition made to court of Magistrate Johnny Meade)

Magistrate: State your case against this man, Mrs. Phillip.

Imelda: Money my is where, man?

Magistrate: Address the Bench, Mrs. Phillip, we don't have all day.

Imelda: Me maintain wouldn't man this.

Magistrate: I beg your pardon?

Imelda: Me maintain not would husband my, say I! Rum on money his all spend he!

Magistrate: Woman, come straight or dismiss will I this case!

Imelda: Mad you! Missdis! Hell much so see me make man this after!

Magistrate: Woman, I can't make head nor tail of what you saying. Mr. Phillip, you does talk backwards too? Oh hoh! What you have to say for yourself?

Spoiler: Your Honour, this is the off-season for calypso and I
can't afford to pay a cent. Not that I don't have the
money, but is the getting.

Magistrate: Explain yourself, young man.

Spoiler: (MONEY IN THE BANK)
My cousin died many years in Toco   }
And he leave a lot of money for Spoilo} Repeat
Now people saying that I lousy
Saying that the Spoiler don't spend his money
But if they put the world in a pitch oil tin
I cannot even pay a cent to see the thing spin

Chorus:
Just because I have my money in the bank
since the age of nine
And them big shots put theirs on mine
I have to wait again just a couple years
In order to get out mine, they have to take off theirs

Friends sometime I wake in the morning
I know I have my money but it's the getting
Run down the road and friend with a taxi
I say that I going and collect currency
Reach in the bank speaking to the cashier
From left to right she shaking she finger
Go away Mr. Phillip no sense you stop
Your money is about two feet six from the top

I pull so much strings I pull cable wire
To see if they could move my money from centre
Stand up by the bank sometimes for a fortnight
Wetting in the rain drying in the sunlight
One day the cashier send and she call me

I say well today Spoiler have some money
But instead of money she say Mr. Thorne
Just put another thousand on top and gone

Is no sense to worry and go half crazy
More patience than Job I could take it easy
Some have they cars to go Pt. Cumana
But I am going to ride on my wooden scooter
Some have they big fat turkey for Christmas
But when the day come I must eat a breakfast
I done accustom let me continue
To live on vaseline and camphor ball stew

Magistrate: That's all well and good but just not good enough.
You must find a way to support your wife. Even one
who talks backward. Pay the $45 or take
two weeks in jail. Next!

Imelda: All is that? Alpagat a like face judge that!

Bro Willie: *(Takes stand)*

Prosecutor: (RAMGOAT BAPTISM)
If you is a Baptist well pray for him
Because I feel that the man committed a sin
Brother Willie, pray for him
Because I feel the man committed a sin
Between the mangrove down in the swamp
Oops Lord they pick up that boldface scamp
Luckily Mr. Haba search for food in the Labasse
And hear when the poor goat blast

Chorus:
Meh eh eh, Brother Willie } Repeat
It was a preacher in the mang

With a candle in his hand
Giving a ramgoat baptism

Maco   That morning I was down in town
Maisey: Busy like a bee but nothing to come
Christmas Eve not a cent in hand
So I run down on the Labasse searching for ham
I get some onion and potatoes
A few heads of cabbage and some ochroes
So then I dump these in my bag
And went searching for crab then I heard
the ballad.

Chorus:

Aha, the goat like a lamb
And the preacher with a big candle in his hand
Brother Willie going wild
If you see how the gentleman making style
Simi dimi and shipshanti for so
And if you hear him with this eku, eku o
When Willie push him in the stream
He realise what he was in Ramgoat start to scream

Chorus:

Bro Willie: The day of the case
You could imagine how people flock up the place
Brother Willie from Tableland
Yes sir yes sir yes sir I am the man
My honour this ramgoat got too much sin
Just how he smelling just so he doesn't pass a thing
He butting his mammy, his granny, he shooting
butt for me
Baptism good for he

Magistrate: Bro. Willie, it have prisoners just waiting for the likes of you to join them. Sixty days hard labour!

Bro Willie: Have mercy, your Honour!

Magistrate: Beeehaah! Next!

Bolt: *(Takes stand)*

Magistrate: *(Reading)* Roy Celestine alias 'Bolt' steelbandsman, and badjohn, am I right? Well, I fed up with you steelbandsmen. You all not content with thiefing people dustbin and noise making, no, you all have to be fighting too.

Bolt: Your honour.........

Magistrate: Silence! Does the Prosecution have anything to add to these charges? If the jail had room, I put the whole of Tokyo steelband in there!

Prosecutor: With the Court's leave I have two witnesses, to call Your Honour, as to what happened on that fateful day.

Magistrate: Proceed.

Prosecutor: Miss Muriel Prim to the stand!

Ms. Prim: (STEELBAND CLASH)
It was a bachannal, ah ha
Fifty carnival, ah ha
Fight for so with Invaders and Tokyo
My friend run and left his hat
When they hit him a baseball bat
Never me again
To jump up in a steelband in Port of Spain

Tokyo in town, ah ha
Blanca coming down, ah ha
If you see how them saga girls dancing round
And friends when the thing get sweet
Lord, Blanca left the street
Never me again
To jump up in a steelband in Port of Spain

Bottle start pelting, ah ha
If you see sledge passing, ah ha
Husband and wife
Look they start running for they life
An Indian man selling bread
Shout out Lord today I dead
Never me again
To jump up in a steelband in Port of Spain

Well the thing get hot, ah ha
If you see men get cut, ah ha
Lord Blakie run in a house by a lady
Quite under the lady bed
They pelt a bottle and buss (his) head
Never me again
To jump in a steelband in Port of Spain

Magistrate: Can't say I blame you at all Miss....

Prim: Prim, Your Honour.

Magistrate: Prim, is it? Quite appreciate your reasoning, if I may
say so. Have you ever given thought to a career in law?

Prim: Me? Law, your Honour? No, sir.

Magistrate: I daresay you have the background for it. It would
be my honour to introduce you to the subject. Let's

say, my chambers in a few minutes?

That's all for today. *(To Prosecutor)* Well, Caruth, sum up and be quick about it.

Prosecutor: (OL' TIME CAT O' NINE)
The only thing to stop these hooligans   }
From causing panic in the island   } repeat
Well I hear that the Government
Feel they need another kind of punishment
I say one thing to cool down this crime
Is to bring back the ol' time cat o'nine

Chorus:
With the ol' time cat o'nine
Beat them bad and they bound to change their mind
Is to send them Carrera with licks like fire
And they bound to surrender

In the days of Judge Gilchrist as you know
Nothing never happen so
Any man pass under his hand
Can tell you of the rod of correction
He use to make them meek and mild
Well, he never spare the rod to spoil the child
I say one thing to cool down this crime
Is to lash them with the ol' time cat o nine.

Magistrate: The Court accepts your submission. You, Mr. Celestine will spend the next twelve months as Her Majesty's guest and receive twelve strokes.

Bolt: What? I giving you a living!

Magistrate: Restrain this man! What do you mean you giving me a living? I'll have you charged with contempt!

Bolt: (NO CRIME NO LAW)
          The government of every country
          Should pay a criminal a big salary
          And when they   commit a crime
          The law wouldn't give them any long time
          The police should be glad when one break a door
          Lock a neck, buss a face or break open a store
          They should be merry when somebody violate the law
          For that is what the government is paying them for

          Chorus:
          And if somebody don't buss somebody face
          How the policeman going to make a case?
          And if somebody don't dig out somebody eye
          The Magistrate will have nobody to try
          And if somebody don't kill somebody dead
          All the judges going to beg their bread
          So when somebody cut off somebody head
          Instead of hanging they should pay them money instead

Magistrate: Restrain, I said, restrain that man! *(This is done with great difficulty before Bolt is taken off)*

Police: Your Honour, your Honour, there's one more case, sir.

Magistrate: Court is adjourned for the day. I have certain pressing matters. Keep the accused in custody until tomorrow. *(Police approaches bench. Takes hold of Magistrate).*

Magistrate: Unhand me, sir! What's the meaning of this?

Police: Well, you is the accused, your Honour, and you say to detain the accused in custody.

Magistrate: Is this some kind of joke?

Police: This warrant your Honour is for speeding at 2:00
          a.m. in the morning of June 15th along the area
          known as the Gaza Strip.

Magistrate: Oh, that old charge. Don't go into details officer.
          May as well get it over with.

Spoiler: (MAGISTRATE TRY HIMSELF)
          Well this one is class   }
          They charge a magistrate for driving too fast } repeat
          But is one courthouse in the district
          He's the only magistrate there to run it
          If you see how the people flock up the place
          To see how the magistrate go try he own a case

          Chorus:
          Himself tell himself you are charged for speeding
          Himself start to shout the policeman lying
          Himself tell himself don't shout, this ain't no sport
          And he charge himself for contempt of court

          He said go ahead
          Lemme hear what happen so the police said
          Sir, if you see how this man could speed
          And he pointing at the magistrate Johnny Meade
          The magistrate ask him who he talking bout
          Is you, him, I mean, the policeman shout out
          The magistrate then pick up a looking glass
          And ask himself is it true your were driving fast?

          Chorus

          Then Mr. Caruth
          He came up and started to prosecute
          The magistrate then call his lawyer
          To defend the defendant who is your honour

And all the time that the lawyer talking
The magistrate serious, sometime he laughing
A time the magistrate tell he ownself, look
I have a great mind to take way your licence book

Chorus

Yes, I nearly drop
When the man take out he pen and start to sum up
I start to study
If he going to put his own self in custody
I was wrong because again he took out the mirror
He self told heself to pay twenty dollar
He buss out a cry, he turn round and say
'Gimme a chance, I want a lil time to pay'

Himself told himself you are charged for speeding
Himself told himself the policeman lying
Himself told himself alright, I will be kind
I giving you five years to pay the fine.

Act 2

Scene II

Ribero: I wash my hands. Friends? Rascals! Where Ming and Figskin? Like Kitch wife. Vanish!

Spoiler: Well, you call your place Wonders Never!

Ribero: Who would believe is you this fete was supposed to help. I sing my throat sore and while I taking my encore, they gone with the gate!

Spoiler: Is only money. It don't last. Friendship mean more.
Anyway, I not in the lock up.

Ribero: Not me and calypsonians again. Ever.

Kitch: When all you miss Kitch, I gone too.

Ribero: Well, till tomorrow.

Kitch: I mean gone, vamoos, abroad. Trinidad ain't have
nothing for calypsonians.

Spoiler: Yankees gone with the money.

Ribero: And the women. If you going New York Kitch, I
have a brother with a rumshop twice as big as this.

Kitch: He ain't getting my money. New York is the last
place I want to see right now.

Spoiler: England?

Kitch: I get a offer for Aruba and Curacao. After that any
number could play.

Spoils: You go make it. You is the best in the business.

Kitch: What 'bout you? The case call yet?

Spoiler: Boy, I so thinking 'bout this case I done dream
courthouse already. I tell you down to the magistrate
name and all. The man is the image of Ribero.
I see the whole thing natural, natural.

Ribero: Me as magistrate? Next time dream me a millionaire!
Wife worries! Leave me single!

Spoiler: Don't worry Kitch, it could be worse. At least your
wife gone with a man; my brother-in-law lose my
sister to a cat!

Kitch: A cat!

Spoiler: Meow, meow.

Ribero: Spoiler, again.

Spoiler: I must make you laugh.

(CAT BRAIN)
Well my sister was suffering with she brain}
And went for operation in Port of Spain   } Repeat
Well the doctor took the brain right out
of my sister head
For wickedness put in the cat own instead
And the brain she had he put it right insideof the kitty
So she turn the cat and the cat turn she

Chorus:
Well in the night is when the trouble start
She up and down the house
Ramsackling the bedroom looking for mouse
And the cat wha' have she brain
He cozy on the bed
Bussing kiss on top of she husband head

When my mother lay the table with the rice and beef
The tomatoes the eddoes and salad leaf
The cat would sit down on the chair of course
And in cat language he calling for pepper sauce
That time my sister ain't business with no table at all
She only looking for the few grains of rice that fall

Otherwise she in the kitchen with another ugly cat
Bussing down those cockroach beetle and rat

One day I see my sister not looking well
What was wrong with her friends I couldn't tell
She only vomiting and creeping under the bed
The girl getting so fat I say she go dead
Well a morning I couldn't watch my nieces and nephews
If you see kitten lying down inside my shoes
Well my mother say she going down Venezuela
She can't afford to be no kitten grand mother

Sales: (GLORY MAMA GLORY)
Glory mama glory, glory mama glory

Ribero: What confusion is this now? This fella does only
keep away customers.

Kitch: That apostrophe of a lunatic!

Sales: It is never too late, brothers and sisters to resist the
sweet beckonings of sin and turn off onto this road,
the road of light and eternal salvation. We welcome
our newest believer. He followed a path that brought
him not only to the doors of the hospital but to the
very portals of perdition. I retrieved him brothers
and sisters and took charge of his worldly goods.
We welcome tonight Brother Figskin.

Spoiler: Who Figskin? We Figskin?

Ribero: Figskin, oui. So that is where all the money gone!
And the crook have the gall to come under my club?

Sales: You there! Barman! Send down a bottle for the
ceremony!

Kitch: Well if you did write and tell me this in England,
I wouda say it was a Spoiler fantasy.

Figskin: (JUST DEY)
Well a domestic servant from San Souci   }
Meet me on the beach last Sunday   } Repeat
I put in a little old talk
She agreed and so we started to walk
But when I met the first mile post
A car came up and ask   us if we want a drop

Chorus:
(She say) Don't worry to take any taxi Figs
It ain't far I going just dey
I does walk this journey home almost every day
It ain't far look is right dey
Well I walk a mile and a half again
This time well my back in pain
But to every mile post that I past she go say
It ain't far again just dey

I always hear how these Toco girls can walk
I didn't believe the talk
Man she take off that day just like Ashe
I fighting my way
Partner when I meet a mile and a half
I couldn't even spot the craft
My eyes get dark my body in pain
And I perspiring like rain

Chorus

Well I walk till I met the Government school
Panting like any mule
But the woman with her deceitful speech

Darling we almost reach
A giddiness held me and I fall
I wake up in the hospital
When I revive the nurse say the doctor say
I was still twenty miles away

Tina: *(At Tina's)* Only full of mouth! Ma Popo, when I put the pressure on so, the gentleman faint.

Popo: Is the food. These town people like they don't know what next to eat. When it ain't talkarie roti, is chow mein. How they expect to maintain their strength eating other people food?.

Tina: Gosh, I clean forget the time, yes. I just ask madam for the half hour to see you off.

Popo: Come girl, pull this thing for me before you leave. *(Corset)*

Tina: How you fare with Kitch?

Popo: He eye on me property in Toco. Say he want to meet my family, but I know is the property he mean. Anyway we going back by diesel.

Tina: Girl, I ain't enjoy myself so for a long time. I sorry you not staying longer.

Popo: You know, time is what I don't have.

Tina: I forget about you and this death talk. How you taking it so cool Gran Gran?

Popo: What else I must do? You town people take on things too much. The secret of youth my dear is waltzing your worries away.

(NEVER WORRY)
The people going about today
Don't realise that worry don't pay} repeat
Resting their worries upon your shoulder
Only bringing you older and older
These wicked things these people does do
They don't realise you have worries too.

Never ever worry, don't mind how things looking hard
Never ever worry, don't mind how you suffering bad
Never ever worry, what I saying is true
Always consider somebody suffering more than you.

This one happen a few weeks ago
Which part quite down at Toco
A fellar wanted to commit suicide
You know he ran quite down by the bayside
Only a fig the man had to eat
Eat the fig and throw the fig skin in the street
By the time the fig skin fall by his feet
A fellar snatch it up and started to eat

Ming: *(Off)* (DIESEL LADY SHAW)
Greng, greng, greng, greng, greng, graw   }
I mean the diesel lady shaw   } repeat

Well afuss me girl friend fraid
She wouldn't travel by the train unless the children
got on shades
She say this is a modern world
No engine on the line should burn charcoal
So much oil in Trinidad
And the poor people needing coal so bad
So in all the engines we prefer
Give me the diesel lady shaw

Popo: That must be Kitch now.

Tina: *(Opens door to Ming with flowers)* She coming now.

Ming: For Bernice, I could wait a hundred years.

Tina: You ain't have long again. *(Exits)*

Popo: *(Screened)* Hi, honeybunch, you reach early.

Ming: Every moment without you is torture. You come
like the Mona Lisa. The more I see you, the more
I want to see.

Popo: I have something special for you today.

Ming: Now or when we reach Toco?

Popo: Come and see it.

Ming: A small comb? What I doing with that?

Popo: Let me show you, toonkooloonks.

Ming: (AH, BERNICE) *(Duet)*
Ah, Bernice don't call me so   }
I don't like it, I want you know   } repeat
When you call me all this sweetname stupidness
And you leave me and you gone I stop dotish
Well darling you will give me misery
Hear the sweet names that Bernice calling me

Keetch, come go to bed
I have a small comb
To scratch your head

Keetch, don't make me cry
You know I love you
You playing shy.

Popo: *(Emerges with comb, singing chorus. During their dance her wig tumbles)*

Ming: A wig? How your head so ..... white?

Popo: Make-up, nuh. I thought I tell Tina fix this thing good for me.

Ming: You looking.............. different.

Popo: Is me, sweetiepie, without all this set of stupidness. *(Removing make-up, etc.)*

Ming: Oh los! You is Bernice?

Popo: The same sweetums, toonkooloonks, chunkanks from last night, Kitch.

Ming: I did mean to tell you, me ain't Kitch. My name is Ming Foo and I married long time. I go see you!

Popo: What about the property in Toco? You don't want it again?

Ming: Keep it for Kitch! *(Dives for door, with Popo in pursuit)*

Popo: Kitch or Ming, you is mine!

Scene III

Spoiler: *(At Ribero's)* (CAKE-STICKING)
A wedding reception is a nice nice thing }
But they have a right to cut out the }
cake sticking } Repeat
The other day I took my wife to a wedding
And they called on she for cake sticking
I growl like a tiger when I see she
Sticking the cake with a feller nicer than me

Chorus:
If he kiss she on she cheek for about half second
I can understand
But the man he hugging and kissing Like chewing
gum stick on
To a warm piece of iron

Some husbands will agree deceitfully
For they wife to go and stick the cake with Harry
That time they grinding like a sugar mill
An' fuss they angry yes they want to kill
Don't talk bout if the feller is a better kisser
They fouti collapse there with yellow fever
More fever friends yes this ain't no fun
When he finish with she all she lipstick gone

The other day at my tantie Puncie wedding
Don't talk about they had a nice gathering
They call on a man they call Mr. Blake
And another feller woman to stick the cake
The feller believe he didn't have reason
Jump off he chair and say never happen
Put me out if you like this is foolishness
Let he get he own girl if he want to kiss

No joke I making I want you believe
The next wedding I go to with my wife name Eve
I feel they go put she out of the place
Because she wearing a iron mask on she face
And if they call on she for cake sticking
No objection friend no joke I making
When the feller going to kiss he wouldn't be fresh
He will be kissing the iron and not she flesh

Ribero: How you dream up them things, Spoilo?
'Chewing gum stick on to hot iron'?

Spoiler: That is joke to when them Yankee hold on to your girl. Ask Kitch.

Ribero: 'When he finish with she, all she lipstick gone.'

Spoiler: No lie. The doctor say I have a 'overactive imagination.'

Ribero: What that mean?

Spoiler: It mean he think I mad, but I know he mad.

Ribero: Try as I might, I can't come up with a new idea.

Spoiler: Ain't you say you done with calypso?

Ribero: With Kitch gone and Figs and Ming not around, I thinking I could try my hand again.

Spoiler: Look, I make a calypso give you. *(Passes copy book page)*

Ribero: 'Rum Bacchanal'?

Spoiler: You is a bartender, not so?

Ribero: How it go?

Spoiler: You want me tell you everything? If you like it, turn
                the words round in your mouth till you find the tune.

Ribero: I like it.   A drink on the house.

Spoiler: That worth at least two bottles.

Ribero: You crazy! You really want Ribero buss. Times
                tough. Start with a petit quart.

Ribero: *(Plays around coming up with . . .)*
                (RUM BACCHANAL)
                Rum bacchanal hear rum confusion
                Vat 19 call Mount Gay a small island
                Mt. Gay say you fresh and you can't tell me such
                He run and call Scotch Liquor, Liberty and Top Notch
                I felt so shame to see Four Barbadians
                Want to fight one Trinidadian

                Chorus:
                So Mountain Dew jump in the brew, waypa
                You fight up with Vat you fight me too
                Be careful how you lashing me, partner
                The razor in my hand I go spoil me character

Spoiler: *(Pulls hat over his face, sleeps)*

Ribero: How that sound? Spoils, Spoiler!
                (Shaking him) Time to close, man. Out like a light
                again. Well another night you have to spend at the
                bar, my friend. No wonder you so versed in the
                law. Tomorrow maybe you finish this, eh? *(Place bottle
                and glass on counter. Locks up. Exits.)*

Chorus: (LAST TRAIN)
Is the last train to San Fernando
The last train to San Fernando
And if you miss this one
You'll never get another one
The last train to San Fernando

Bolt: *(Enters by forcing a window. Surveys room,
sleeper, goes behind counter. Searches in annoyance)*
Shit! A baseball bat and rum!

Spoiler: *(Sits bolt upright)* No chaser!

Bolt: *(Panics, ducks under bar)*

Spoiler: Somebody just offer me a drink? Or was I dream-
ing? *(Noticing darkness)* You mean Ribero lock me
inside again? He think I living nowhere? I go kick
hell after I take this steadier. *(Going to bar, pours heavy
drink)*

Bolt: *(Moves around. Springs, locking his neck)*

Spoiler: Lord, is Spoils, Ribero! I go pay for the drink!

Bolt: Spoiler the calypsonian?

Spoiler: Lord, it ain't Ribero!

Bolt: Shut up! Before I break you neck like a fowl foot!

Spoiler: I shut up.

Bolt: I ask if you is Spoiler the calypsonian?

Spoiler: Himself, but ease up on the neck lil bit, nuh.

Bolt: You best don't bawl here tonight.

Spoiler: I can't even breathe.

Bolt: *(Releases him)* You know me?

Spoiler: Too dark.

Bolt: Good. *(Back to counter)* Where he does keep it?

Spoiler: Ribero don't leave no money here.

Bolt: The gun! Where he does keep he gun?

Spoiler: Gun? *(Laughs)* You let that ol talk fool you? The only gun Ribero have is gun talk. He does keep that old baseball bat a Yankee fella give Gaza and Gaza.....

Bolt: You lying as usual? This ain't no Mickey Mouse picture, you know.

Spoiler: Look for yourself. If he had a gun where else he would keep it?

Bolt: *(After a pause)* A blasted baseball bat. I mad lick off Ribero head! Anyhow even with this I go be ready for them Invaders boys.

Spoiler: You is a steelband man? Take my stupid advice. That war that brewing between allyou, somebody go pay heavy for it. Why allyou must fight, fight so all the time?

Bolt: What you know about anything except to drink rum and sing rubbish? Your days done, man. You was no use to nobody before and you is less now.

Spoiler: You know me?

Bolt: *(Hard silence)*

Spoiler: What you say is true, though. I never had much use.
But I never like violence. Nobody go respect all you.

Bolt: Look at where respect have you.

Spoiler: The magistrate go los' you in jail.

Bolt: They go have to catch me first and you ain't go be
talking.

Spoiler: You go darken the Spoils? I done give you me word,
I ain't go tell a soul.

Bolt: Your word *(laughs)* that worth even less than your
advice. If my mother did wait on your word, we
starve to death. At least I live to fight
steelband war. You know who I is now?

Spoiler: Wait, you is ....am...

Bolt: Yeah, I is 'ahm'. Now you know why you ain't go
be talking. *(Moves to exit)*

Spoiler: Wait. At least let me see how you look.

Bolt: Touch that switch and I break your blasted hand!

Spoiler: Take it easy, son.

Bolt: Don't call me that! I is just another steelbandman
and to me you is just another calypsonian. Remember that.

Spoiler: You heading for trouble, boy.

Bolt: I born in trouble, grow in trouble.

Spoiler: John Wayne in Pittsburg'. Only thing that was just a picture.

Bolt: Yeah, but this bat in my hand real though. You want to feel it?

Spoiler: Is alright.

Bolt: Feel it. Let we suppose is a picture in truth. Suppose I is who you think I is, what you feel I should do with you?

Spoiler: Life don't always turn out how we want it.

Bolt: And how you woulda want it? Supposing this and supposing that, let we suppose you coulda change it.

Spoiler: Kaiso is my life, boy. I could stop drinking, done with that, but my singing will stop only when I stop breathe. Longer, because life itself ain't much. You is king today, tomorrow you less than dust. But I don't just 'suppose', I does compose. You know what that is, boy? I does make memories that in misery, ketcharse or pain could still bring a little light, a little smile to some old beat-up life. To you that mightn't be much, but is what I does do and I does it damn well.

Bolt: Not good enough.

Spoiler: Because you too vex with the world to laugh?

Bolt: Because all them memories mean nothing to
               nobody. Tomorrow your words gone with the wind.

Spoiler: People go remember, man, they must remember. Not
               the lives, but the love, the songs, they go remember.

Bolt: See for yourself. I gone.   *(House lights)*

Spoiler: They'll remember .... they'll remember.
               But it still so dark.......*(struggles through song, expecting
               audience to know it)*

               (MY SHADOW)
               Partner yes I want to know
               Tell me why my shadow does get on so
               Spoiler want to know
               Tell me why my shadow does get on so
               Because when I wake in the morning
               If I only scratch is my shadow scratching
               I go to 'hosay maday' I telling you
               And as I lift up my hand he lift he own too

Chorus: I vex I really vex yes I want to know
               Tell me why my shadow does get on so
               I make a joke and I kiss my neighbour donkey
               And my shadow kissing too mocking me

               Partner, I ain't making fun
               If you ain't have a shadow don't pray to get one
               Your private affairs
               You discussing that he cocking he ears
               Don't mind you bathe him down with hot water
               He there, he there, he there bet you gold and silver
               All efforts you try you compel to fail
               You come like the magnet and he the nail

Partner but Mr. Wilfred
He tell me how to cut off my shadow head,
Oh mi darling He say half pass nine
Go and put my head on top the train line, Oh Lord
And when I hear the train coming
Don't move my head just welcome the engine
That's all I have to do and I feel he right
So my head on the train line tomorrow night

Chorus: *(At a graveside)*
Name the next singer
His stories frank yet laced with humour
His Hindi songs brought him fame
Like Indian Girls with Them Creole Names

Killer: (GREEN FOWL)
Big trouble with a rooster that I had   }
And a parrot where I live in Fyzabad   } repeat
You know I never see that since I born
I had to stop giving any rooster corn
The drake new in the yard, rooster kill he dead
And now like he planning to capture me parrot head

Chorus:
The parrot say, be careful, be careful, be careful
How you getting on when you belly full
For if you rush me as the duck you go get your death
Because I sure that you never see a green fowl yet

Every morning and evening where I living
Me neighbours complaining
Lord, sometimes 'bout them pigeons
Or them little baby chickens just born
What a funny rooster
He ain't passing nothing once it got feathers

I stand up in the yard, I watch till I fall
But when he karray at the parrot, the parrot bawl

Big trouble that I had last Saturday
With a turkey that I bought from Garroway
You know how these turkeys big and strong
You should see how my rooster knock him down
A child in the yard crying out 'Daddy!
Come and see how the rooster kill the turkey!'
The parrot upstairs he watching everything
And when the bacchanal done he start to laugh
and sing

You fix up, you fix up properly
Last time it was duck, this time is turkey
But when you come at me you go get your bet
For I sure that you never see a green fowl yet!

Chorus: Now this next singer
His name to the world he will soon declare
But just in case he buss
We want you to help him sing the chorus.

Commander: (MR. ACTION)
Give me name a ease
The Commander begging the public please
Give me name a ease
Mr. Action begging the public please
To be a parakeet ain't nice bad
For me to break a warrant it must be hard
Why? Anywhere I go it is just de same
All where I pass you could hear them calling my name

Mr. Action, what you say?
How she going? You O.K.?

Nice! Right away!
And so they calling up me name for the
whole damn day!

I does want to dead
Everyday is the same old tune in my head
And is a thing I don't like at all
Anywhere I pass for my name to call
You could believe it or not but is a certainty
It ain't have a thing I hate like publicity
And the thing they want eats me and gets me angry
They only calling my name unnecessary

Mr. Action, what you say?
How she going? You O.K.?
Nice! Right away!
A man can't walk in peace on the damn highway

When I does wonder if they own jaw bone ain't weary
Whole day so they only bothering me
Sometimes I hear them but I wouldn't answer at all
Well is now me poor name they will call and bawl
If I did owe the government I must a get hold
I don't know how me poor name ain't catch a
lining cold
These people they really got good constitution
I ain't know how some of them ain't got consump-
tion

Mr. Action, what you say?
How she going? You O.K.?
Nice! Right away!
Man I fed up with them on the damn highway

Chorus: This one real easy
You ain't even need no long memory

By now you must get the rake
Who sing this song in Ma Popo wake?

Wrangler: (TOCO WAKE)
Big big wake up in Toco
Was the death of Ma Popo
Lord I went to a wake up in Toco
Was the death of Ma Popo
That night my prayer book tear in piece
A woman snatch me like a police
Bawling come jump up in the ring
Time to prove yourself a bongo King

Tonight is the bongo night
Vine way, vine way Bongo
Bongo messi don ya
Vine way vine way Bongo
Jackass go laugh and talk
Vine way, vineway Bongo, vineway

Well the light wasn't a candle
Was oil and cloth in a bundle
And is like if corbeaux had know that
So when man dead was to chant
Music kicking hell in the place
Don't mind a bamboo joint was the base
Man jumping like if is non-stop
Don't care even if they trousers drop

But this one beat everything
Once Sovereign Law went out hunting
He just lose for two days or so
They bawl he dead, they start to bongo
But while the wake going on
He reach back with he four dogs and gun

He was so glad for the break
The man start to bongo in he own wake

Chorus: Ouch? If you getting bite
Don't worry to fuss, don't worry to fight
You are one of the chosen few
It might be Spoiler saying 'I love you'

Spoiler: (BEDBUG)
Yes I heard when you die after burial
You have to come back as some insect   }
or animal   } Repeat
Well if is so I don't want to be a monkey
Neither a goat a sheep or donkey
My brother say he want to come back a hog
But not Spoiler I want to be a bed bug

Chorus: Just because I want to bite them young ladies partner
Like a hot dog or a hamburger
And if you know you thin, don't be in a fright
Is only big fat women that I'm going to bite

What would you like to be I ask Mr. Ross
He say he'll beg the devil to turn him a horse
I ask another feller they call Lawrence
He said he want to be a big black wood ants
They too foolish when you turn a horse
You have to carry people load get licks from your boss
And as a wood ants is old wood you have to eat
But as a bedbug I biting the human meat

Yes I want you believe it so help me bless
I'll be a different kind of bedbug from all the rest
I ain't biting no ordinary people
You have to be quite social and respectable

Such as female doctors and barristers
Duchesses princesses with nice figures
And when I bite them friends I going and boast
And I calling myself King Bedbug the first

Yes I know some husbands how they fast and fresh
They will be waiting for the Spoiler to bite they flesh
But I wouldn't bite a man if they kill me dead
Not as long as the opposite sex on the bed
Biting a man I might break my teeth
To a bed bug man skin harder than concrete
So if a bug bite a man the result is bad
Man foot have too much hair and they leg too hard

All: (YOUNG BRIGADE SONG) *(Exit)*
Young brigade again
We young and we got the brain
Tell them we ain't fraid
We go mash up the Old Brigade.

Curtain

Calypsoes of the 1950s - 1960s)

Characters

Sparrow — King Of Calypso

Johnny Wright — White (English Creole) Businessman And Property Owner.

Melody — Calypsonian

Tants — A Businesswoman

Blakie — Calypsonian

Goldteeth — Steelband Captain, Badjohn And Friend Of Sparrow

Second Spring — Prostitute

Lulu — Helper And Waitress At Tantie's Teashop (East Indian Descent)

Dr. Paul — Newspaper Vendor / M.c.

Dr. Eric Williams — Chief Minister, Later Prime Minister Of Trinidad And Tobago

Jean Smith — Carnival Queen (Also White)

Jean Marabunta — Prostitute

Elaine — Prostitute

Delamonte — Christo, Calypsonian

Kitchener — Calypsonian, Also Road March Champion

List Of Calypsoes (In Order)

Act I

SLAVE -Sparrow
WILLIAM THE CONQUEROR -Sparrow
JONAH AND THE BAKE -Melody
ARABIAN FESTIVAL -Blakie
MAMA LOOK AH BOO BOO -Melody
MR. MELODY -Melody
JEAN AND DINAH -Sparrow
MISS SWEDEN -Christo
PNM VICTORY -Striker
SHAKE YOUR BALISIER -Cypher
LULU -Sparrow
KEEP THE CITY CLEAN -Sparrow
BRASS CROWN -Superior
SMARTMAN MELO -Sparrow
SPARROW SISTER - Melody
NO DOCTOR NO -Sparrow
PEDDLARS -Melody
CHICKEN CHEST -Christo
CARNIVAL BOYCOTT -Sparrow
THE BASE -Sparrow
GUNSLINGERS -Sparrow
RUN THE GUNSLINGERS -Caruso
DON'T BLAME THE PNM -Striker
REPLY TO MELODY -Sparrow
SPARROW UGLY TOO -Melody
MADAME DRACULA -Sparrow
BELMONT JACKASS -Melody
GRENADIANS -Blakie
TEN TO ONE IS MURDER -Sparrow

Act II

ROBBERY WITH V - Sparrow
DON'T COME BACK AGAIN -Kitchener
MOCK DEMOCRACY -Christo
BWIA SONG -Christo
DISCRIMINATION -Melody
SHAME AND SCANDAL -Melody
NO MORE ROCK AND ROLL -Sparrow
FEDERATION -Sparrow
THE ROAD -Kitchener
LOVE AND MISS DOVE -Cypher
MAMA DIS IS MAS -Kitchener
BAD IMPRESSION -Kitchener
NO MORE CALYPSONG -Kitchener
MR. KITCHENER -Sparrow
TRINIDAD IS COOL AND QUIET -Kitchener
OUTCAST -Sparrow
BORN TO BE-Caruso
MASSA DAY -Chalkdust
BLACK IS BEAUTIFUL -Duke
TEN TO ONE IS MURDER -Sparrow

NB: The 'Massa Day Done' Speech (p.171) is an abridged version of the Speech delivered by Prime Minister, Eric Williams in 1961.

Prologue

A chorus of dancers in the calypso THE SLAVE. *performed by the band or recorded. They are the people of the play - prostitutes, panmen, badjohns, the underclass of Port of Spain.*

(THE SLAVE)
I'm a slave from a land so far   }
I was caught and I was brought here   }
from Africa.   } repeat
It was licks like fire from the white slave master
Everyday I down on me knees
Weeks and weeks before we cross the seas
To reach in the West Indies.

Chorus:
And then they make me work
Oh yes I work
Good Lord no pay
And I toil and toil and toil and toil so hard each day
I'm dying, I'm crying,
O Lord, I want to be free.

In my heart there was much to say
And I hope that the boss would listen to me someday
Although he knew my request was small
It was the sting of the whip there to answer me
when I call.
We had to chant and sing to express our feeling
To that wicked and cruel man.
That was the only medicine to make him listen
And is so Calypso began.

The dance crescendoes on 'Ah Wanna Be Free'. *From this tableau a figure emerges as the news spreads:* 'The Doc, The Doc, he coming' *The chorus becomes a crowd in a public square in Port of Spain, 1956. The dark-suited figure ascends the speaker's platform. He can fit comfortably into the welcome of a large woman, but if he removed his dark shades she would recoil from the intensity of his eyes.*

Crowd: (WILLIAM THE CONQUEROR)
Praise little Eric, rejoice and be glad
We have a better future here in Trinidad
P.N.M, it ain't have nobody like them
For we have a champion leader
William the Conqueror.

Williams: Tonight I shall explain to you fully just what is meant when I say Massa Day done. What was Massa Day the Massa Day that is done? Who is Massa? Massa was more often that not an absentee European planter exploiting West Indian resources, both human and economic. Massa's economic programme was to grow sugar and nothing but sugar. The West Indian Massa constituted the most backward ruling class history has ever known. If the people prefer Massa to the PNM - then they have a democratic right to make a history that will be unique in the world. History is full of instances where slave owners restore slavery or try to restore slavery. I know of no instance when the slaves themselves, once emancipated, return voluntarily to their former chains. And so we proceed to the election bearing aloft proudly our banner of interracial solidarity, with the slogan described thereon 'Massa Day Done, Sahib Day Done, Yes Suh Boss Day Done!'

Exits away from crowd who disperse repeating song.
Tantie's teashop. She snaps off a radio.

Tants: Hm! I smelling trouble. Lulu! That callaloo off the stove?

Lulu: I still swizzling it, Tantie.

Tants: Swizzling your little tail. Girl, burn my pot and I pack your backside back Carapo in one go. Look, give me that stick. Go now and clean down the counter.

Lulu: Tants, is true what the Doctor say about the white wickedness in the days of slavery?

Tants: What stupidness you asking me, chile? For your information I was never a slave and I have no doctorship in History. But common sense alone tell me put a whip in any man hand and he will use it. I watching this thing. That Dr. Paul and all of them who jumping up at meeting is when they feel the whip on their back, they will know who is the real massa. *(Melody and Blakie come along the street with Second Spring in tow)* Do fast, chile! Time to serve. My customers coming, belly in hand.

Melody: (JONAH AND THE BAKE)
Well, a Baptist test living peacefully   }
With four little children in Laventille   } repeat
His work was selling sweepstake
So one evening he roast up some bake
Went to sleep and get up a bake missing
So he wake the children and started asking

Chorus
Jonah! Yes, Pa?

You take a bake here?
No Pa
One gone, one gone!
Well, the power fly in the old man head
He grab a belt and nearly kill the poor children dead
Wap! Wap, wap, wap! etc.

Tants: You don't have to sing for your supper at Tantie's, Lord Melody. Just point and its yours.

Melody: *(Indicating Tantie)* The hands that cook the sweetest creole food in the whole of Port of Spain.

Tants: Sweetmouth. All calypsonian the same. I know you done order in song. Lulu, bake and buljol by one! Blakie?

Melody: Tants, it have a set of hungry calypsonian up and down the road always looking for trus' but don't trus' them at all. Ay-ay, Blakie, I ain't see you there, partner.

Blakie: Tants, the usual with no tanka bouli.

Melody: Tanka-who?

Tants: Lulu, one cow-heel, no pepper.

Blakie: And I ain't trusting. Melo payin' for two.

Spring: For two? So whappen? I on diet?

Blakie: Woman, we look like Yankee? Why you don't go home and mind your grand children?

Melody: All you calypsonians ain't playing good, nah. What you say? Tankabouli?

Blakie: Check the Arabian dictionary. If you don't know a lil bit of everybody language you can't call yourself a cosmopolitan calypsonian.

(ARABIAN FESTIVAL)
I disguise and I call myself Al Mustapha
Went to a Arab festival in Arabia
For your better information if you want to know
I was the calypsonian they pick to go
But I couldn't speak the language so I ain't rude
But I learn on the way how to beg for food.

Chorus:
Was give me some.....
The menu kill Abdullah the other day.

Spring: Tants, beg you some water please. From today I doing just like the Chinaman when he put up he sign. *(They watch her drink)* 'No Dogs and Calypsonians Allowed' *(Flounces out)*

Blakie: I thought you was going to say 'Hands Wanted'.

Melody: Nigger belly full! Time for kaiso! Blakie, this one is to help you indigest.

(MAMA LOOK A BOO BOO)
I wonder why nobody don't like me   }
Or is it a fact that I'm ugly   } repeat
I leave me whole house and go
Me children don't want me no more
They curse me black is white and thing
And when I talk they start to sing.

Sparrow: *(Entering)* Mama, look a boo-boo, they shout
They mother tell them, 'Shut up your mouth!'

That is your father, 'Oh no,
My daddy can't be ugly so.'

Melody: And who you is, young fella, to cut into a big man song?

Sparrow: Sparrow. I know all your songs by heart.

(MR. MELODY)
'Mr. Melody
Me mother send me
She say if you want the thing, you could get the thing
But first you must give her a ring.'

Melody: *(Joining him)*
'Go back and tell you mama
Tell her for me I'm all alone
Don't forget to tell her the electrician
Came and took the telephone.' *(Laughs)*

Sparrow: You like it? I could sing with you?

Blakie: Hold on, hold on, it don't go so. You ain't even good out your nest yet. Where you sing before? And who give you that name 'Sparrow'?

Sparrow: I born to sing kaiso. Hear this. *(Spring re-enters)*
Jean and Dinah
Rosita and Clementina
Came to me one morning
After they completed their shopping
They told me, Honey
I never had more luxury
More than when I stop
And went to Salvatori to shop.

(Silence) Well, what you think?

Blakie: I think I know somebody who looking for just what you have to offer. I could send you by him now and you get a good ten dollars for that guitar.

Sparrow: This man looking for fight.

Melody: That is a jingle. Why you don't sell it to Salvatori?

Sparrow: I try. Salvatori know about merchandise not music. Want to offer me two dollars.

Blakie: He had nothing smaller?

Melody: Look, come down by the Club, Maple Leaf. Your song ain't much, but I like your spirit. I go talk to the management.

Sparrow: Now you talking. So, how much this Club does pay?

Blakie: Pay? You go be lucky if you even get to sing, and if you do sing is for just what you come inside here for. Macafouchette.

Sparrow: Well, all you could keep that. Me ain't taking nobody left-overs.

Melody: Up to you, but how else you expect people to hear you? You have to start as a helper. In calypso, young fella, it ain't what you get, but what you bring that count. Whatever you is, voice, looks, ability, your story, you, that is the kaiso. *(Intently)* How you shaking so? You frighten?

Sparrow: I ain't go lie, yes. Your face, man....

Melody: Put that in a calypso and we go meet. Down at the Club. *(Exits)*

Blakie: And if you coming, thief a jacket should in case you get to sing.

Sparrow: So what? Jacket does sing now?

Blakie: You see you, you is trouble. I see that already. *(Exits)*

Sparrow: You ever see that, Tantie? You have something to sell, you know it good, but nobody ain't buying?

Spring: My life story.

Tants: Packaging, sonny. If the saltfish not selling, put it in accra. You ordering?

Spring: I must try that.

Tants: Second Spring, this overtime work will kill you out. You ain't find is time you retire?

Spring: I was due for retirement then the Yankees reach and put new life in my blood. I outlast them and all and still looking good. You ain't think so, young fellar?

Sparrow: I ain't think, I ain't guess, I know. Deep down in my soul I know I is a king.

Spring: Kissmearse royalty.

Tants: Listen, young man, dove or pigeon or whatever you call yourself....

Sparrow: Sparrow.

Tants: Idle fantasizing is for the birds is true, but I don't encourage it in my shop. Nothing like a full belly to firm up your prospects. Kitchener always say that and you see how good he doing in England.

Spring: And he was never stingy like these bottom of the barrel bards they have nowadays.

Sparrow: On this empty plate I take this oath, the days of calypso poverty done with this singer. I ain't thiefing, I ain't begging and I ain't going hungry.

Tants: You starting in the right place. So what you having?

Sparrow: Callaloo, and a full plate of calypso. Spring, thanks for the story. I eating them raw down at the Maple Leaf. All who pass through before, Spoiler, Killer, Kitchener, Tiger and Atilla, tell them make way. Sparrow take over now.

(JEAN AND DINAH). *He walks the song from the teashop to the Maple Leaf Club to the Dimanche Gras show, varying pace and delivery to indicate different audiences / locations.*

Scene II

(JEAN AND DINAH)
Well the girls in town feeling bad
No more Yankees in Trinidad
They going to close down the Base for good
Them girls got to make out how they could
Brother, is now they park up in town

In for a penny and in for a pound
Believe me is competition for so
Trouble in the town when the price drop low.

Chorus:
Jean and Dinah
Rosita and Clementina
Round the corner posing
Bet you life is something they selling
And if you catch them broken
You can get it all for nothing
Don't make a row.
The Yankees gone and Sparrow take over now.

It's the glamour boys again
We are going to rule Port of Spain
No more Yankees to spoil the fete
Dorothy have to take what she get
All of them who used to make style
Only taking two shilling with a smile
No more hotel and Simmonds bed
By the sweat of thy brow thou shall eat bread.

MC: Another round of applause for newcomer, the
Mighty Sparrow!   Tonight is the big one ladies and
gentlemen, Dimanche Gras. Who will be Queen of
Carnival? Who the Calypso King? Can Sparrow's
girls outshine this favourite from the Lord Christo?
Miss Sweden !

Christo: (MISS SWEDEN- *After first stanza and Chorus, music
alone under dialogue)*
I was present this year }
Long Beach, California } Repeat
The whole population

Was making preparation
Watching lovely ladies rehearse
A beauty queen contest for Queen of the Universe

Chorus:
Well after all was said and done
You can't deny Miss Sweden won
Ring out three cheers for coming first
Miss Sweden is the Queen of the Universe.

(*Backstage, John Wright is in Jean's dressing room.*)

Jean: I ain't sure I right for this Queen Show business, nuh. How I looking, Mr. Wright?

Wright: Like a queen. Queen Jean. My queen.

Jean: I feeling like a pappyshow, but if you say so.

Wright: Girl, you custom-made, you have it all - colour, class and looks too. How you mean you ain't know? Ask your older sister, auntie, your friend that stage, this show, is we own. Tonight is yours.

Jean: I hope I don't let you down, Mr. Wright.

Wright: Girl, I tell you you done win. I in this business too long to take chances. My only grouse with you is this 'Mr. Wright' talk. You don't like 'Johnny' or what?

Jean: You having a good time, eh, Mr. Wright?

Wright: What the hell, is Carnival ....Carnival '56'! The way it looking, in fact, might be we last good Carnival for a damn long time. Have a good time, yes!

Jean:	Time to go. How these calypsonians taking so long on stage. They ain't know this is a Carnival Queen show?
Wright:	Don't study the calypsonians. Their future out there. Yours here. Gimme a kiss.
Jean:	Mr. Wright, not because you sponsoring me mean I will just do what you want, you know.
Wright:	Oh? So what it mean? Tell me. You think the money I put in this show is just for you to shake your tits in front the Grand Stand?
Jean:	Mr. Wright!
Wright:	Johnny!
Jean:	Johnny.
Wright:	Well? That is what you think?
Jean:	I think this ain't for me. I have my pride.
Wright:	Then take it off. Fling way the costume and walk out the Savannah. The Convent just across the road and the calypsonians still singing. (Pause) For some is the car or the trips and the cash. Others get high on the idea, the conceit. Which type you is? I tell you this ain't no competition Jean, is your inheritance.
MC:	Our big moment, ladies and gentlemen, the Carnival Queen Parade!
Band:	*(Happy Wanderer)*

Wright: Show time. Watch you step, girl, you want to fall?
Even if you fall, what the hell? You done win
already! So shake your tail and show them, show
them you is Queen! Queen Jean! J'ouvert is ours!
and the Carnival is still we own!

Jean: *(Parades the stage to Happy Wanderer. she crosses stage
repeatedly as other 'contestants' are announced.)*

MC: Miss Forgarty's! Miss J. T. Johnson's! Miss
Glendening's! Miss Furness Withy!

Band: *(Flourish)*

MC: And the Calypso King 1956, ladies and gentlemen....

Band: JEAN AND DINAH

Crowd: *(Bearing Sparrow across stage, through audience change chorus
to 'the doctor take over now.')*

Spring: *(With flag PNM VICTORY)*

Chorus:
So when I ask the people which party they voting
They told me the PNM
The young and the old and all little children
Shouting out PNM
They say the government that we had before
They made this a corrupted land
So Big Belly you stick you grind
For your bad administration.

Dr. Paul: *(In Albert Gomes caricature)*
(SHAKE YOUR BALISIER)

24th of September   }
Election day I bound to remember   } repeat
A steelband held up in front me door
Was PNM victory I am sure
Well I came out side to enjoy the fete
When a nurse hold me around me neck.

Chorus:
She said: PNM shake your balisier!
If you see how that lady break away
PNM shake your balisier!
I told her shake if you shaking.

We start from Arima
To meet the next candidate Tunapuna
Red Army was leading
Crossfire behind, imagine how I jumping
The law told us not to drink no rum
So I stop by the police station
The Corporal came out frowning up he face
With a long balisier tie around he waist.

(Transition into Tanties' Shop)

Scene III

Dr. Paul: People, that was bacchanal! And I play a good mas.
Albert Gomes, ex- Chief Minister! 'Big Belly Making
Chile'.

Tants: Woe betide the poor man the people love.

Dr. Paul: From Arima to town, the whole of Trinidad, I tell
you, on the road.

Tants: And where they is now that a good six months pass? Up and down the road half of them, still, looking for work.

Dr. Paul: Six months. How much time is that in the life of a government? Besides, you know how much years of cleaning up they have to do after that last set of crooks?

Tants: Mr. Gomes was a very nice man!

Dr. Paul: Maybe so, but his government was corrupt and incompetent.

Tants: Dr. Paul, I wouldn't have you! Don't feel because you went to two meeting in that University of Woodford Square you could come and parrot about 'corrupt and incompetent'. Milk, rice, sugar sky high, tax in we tail, excuse me, you call that competence?

Dr. Paul: We call that self-government. The Doc say freedom ain't cheap and we paying we way! Massa day done!

Tants: Freedom from what? Youself Dr. Paul, you think before this election anybody man or manicou could come in this teashop and tell me I not free? I would send them skating. Now we paying for freedom that we had long time ?

Dr. Paul: Not that kind of freedom, I mean...

Tants: You mean the expensive kind? The kind other people buy and sell you. Not the kind you born with?

Dr. Paul: Peace.

Lulu: (*Entering*) Sorry I so late Tantie. I get keep back.
Confusion in the yard this morning...

Tants: I don't want to hear 'bout it. Second time this week.
I watching you good. You in town too long.

Dr. Paul: Morning, Lulu.

Lulu: Morning Dr. Paul.

Tants: What is all this morning, morning business? The
Queen of Sheba arrive? Look, your work waiting for
you in the back, and don't forget to wash your hands.
(*Lulu exits*)

Dr. Paul: Indian, Creole, it don't matter. Young people the
same all over.

Tants: That is what this freedom talk bring. Anybody doing
anything they want. The other night, that one, soon
as she finish work, she and that scamp, Sparrow.
Like they did think my ears ain't good.

Sparrow: (LULU *A Duet*)
Come lewwe go Lulu   }
Is a long time I watching you   } Repeat
You're the only woman in Trinidad
I want you so bad I going staring mad
Have no fear the batchey is there
No one can interfere

Lulu: I fraid you make a calypso on me
(Not me) I don't want you to make no calypso on me
I know nobody go see and is only the two of we
But I fraid you go make a calypso on me.

Sparrow: You making skylark, Lulu
I am surprised at you
I give you my word of honour
I want you to remember
I wouldn't mention a word to anyone
What we do we do and what is done is done
Don't destroy my heart like a Christmas toy
Lewwe go and spread some joy.

Lulu: I fraid you make a calypso on me
(Not me) I don't want you to make no calypso on me
I know nobody go see and is only the two of we
But I fraid you go make a calypso on me.

Tants: Lulu! Go where you going! As for you, Mr. Sparrow,
not because you win Calypso King mean every
woman is your prize. You ain't have enough? Leave
the chile!

Sparrow: My intentions honourable, Tants.

Tants: And my name is Belmont Jackass. I know just where
your intentions start and where they stop. But if she
come here with any belly you best find she a work
with you dirty spoats.

Sparrow: Me Tants? I don't meddle with them sort. Me ain't
working rubbish again.

(KEEP THE CITY CLEAN)
I hear they have a new campaign
Cleaning Port of Spain
I know they should really clean up town
But they start so wrong
They only put a few dustbin

On them lampost collect fruit skin
But if they don't want no rubbish in sight
See me and I think I'll put them right

Chorus:
They should hold Marabunta Jean
And they hold Pickey Head Eileen
And then hold Stinking Mouth Doreen
If they want to keep the city clean.

They making so much fuss and thing
About mango skin
Old onion and rotten potato
But like they don't know
Some of them girls they have in town
Sweaty going round
I would rather eat a rotten ham
Than to smell up underneath some of them arm.

Women: *(Emerge from darkness as named propositioning the audience before they approach Sparrow)*

Marabunta: Is lice you like to pick? Don't worry with dry-tail Lulu. A king like you deserve a queen.

Sparrow: Jean Marabunta.

Marabunta: Queen of the streets, my dear. We ain't even celebrate since you win Calypso King with my name.

Elaine: At least you could invite we home to see the fridge and the radio.

Sparrow: Fridge and radio? The Carnival Queen get that. The lil $25.00 I get, what ain't spend, Melo borrow.

Spring: That Melo don't pay back.

Marabunta: Wait. You mean you is Calypso King and all you get
                is that lil cacada?

Spring: And a brass crown that can't even pawn.

Elaine: Boy, we does make more than that on a bad night.
                You ain't shame?

Marabunta: All you calypsonian have so much mouth for
                woman....

Others: When I tell you, mouth!

Marabunta: I hope when the time come all you remember how
                to stand-up!

> (BRASS CROWN) *(Melo enters, joining song)*
> Yes, a calypsonian   }
> Needs more consideration   } Repeat
> Look at the Carnival Queen competition
> And for the King Calypsonian
> Well, the Queen getting everything
> And nothing goes to the Calypso King.
>
> *Chorus:*
> She gets refridgerators
> Machine, radios and even motor cars
> Sometimes a Simmonds bed
> And all the King get is a brass crown on his head.
>
> They take the King Calypso
> To make a pappyshow
> He gets a couple dollars
> And a million pat on his shoulders

What he gets, my friends, is rather small
Is next to nothing at all
But the Queen only puts herself in spot
And after that she becomes a real big shot.

Elaine: Melo darling! Lover boy! What you have for your girls?

Melody: Bad news. My pocket get pick.

Sparrow: Melo, you too lie! That money you borrow from me, I want it.

Melody: For boys like you, the name is Mr. Melody.

Sparrow: Well, pleased to meet you. I is King Sparrow and I want my money.

Melody: King of what? Savannah grass. That brass crown don't mean one mas. The only kingdom boy, is here, in these streets, where man to man, woman to man, have and want does meet. These people self does be judge and jury. That lesson alone worth more than the money you say I borrow, so now you owing me.

Sparrow: You really want me slice you up?

Melody: If you stanza sharp enough. Step three paces back, boy, and let we see if you have skill to match your mouth.

Sparrow: *(Obliging)* (SMARTMAN MELO)
Melody too smart and conniving   }
You must never, never believe him   } Repeat

Look he borrow some money from me
To send for his girl in B.G.
He buy clothes to fill a basket
Now is time to pay me back he say he pocket get pick
(But he lie)

Chorus:
I want me money by tomorrow
You think you have more brain than Sparrow, Melo
No pickpocket will ever try to pick
A next pickpocket pocket (you mustn't lie)
No pickpocket will ever try to pick
A next pickpocket pocket

Melody: Not bad for a beginner, but let me tell all you, when it come to thiefing Sparrow have a sister in a class by she self.

(SPARROW SISTER)
Lemme go, she bawl   }
Shame on you, Melody after all } Repeat
I coulda commit murder
With this thiefing woman from Grenada
Afterwards I get to know
She was the sister of the Sparrow.

Chorus:
This time she carry way me sleeping gown
Me false teeth gone, me inhaler can't be found
Sparrow! Tell your sister Hog Mouth Elaine
She go thief again. (repeat)

Sparrow: If you wasn't my brother-in-law, you know I get damn vex.

Melody: Me and you could be family? I is a peaceful, loving man, you is a badjohn. Hear this one 'bout Sparrow.

Sparrow: Melo, wait. *(To crowd)* All you want to hear this lie Melo going and tell? Well, pay all you money and come in the Club. Melo, why we must be giving way good, good calypso in the street? And fighting over money? Is mauvais langue all you like? Come in the Club and hear how Melody face like a saucepan.

Melody: Is true what you saying, not the part 'bout the saucepan, you son of a catharr - nose Grenadian . . .

Sparrow: What about the baby-cow I see that is you Melo, in print? *(Exit. Crowd following).*

Scene IV

Dr. Paul: *(Enters with sign)* Finish Tants. Where you want it hang?

Tants: Let me see it first. (READS) 'In God We Trus, In Man We Bus'? Is shame you want to bring to me eye? Trust end with 'T' and b-u-r-s-t is burst. They ain't teach all you that in the Square?

Dr. Paul: But nobody ain't go understand what that mean. 'In Man We Burst'? Besides, it don't rhyme.

Tants: Rhyme? Is a calypso I asking you to make? All I want is a little proper English. That is too much, Dr. Paul?

Dr. Paul: Well, you see, sometimes in order to get the message across you does have to bend the rules a little, Doris... if you know what I mean.

Tants: I have one rule. Come straight. That is what that mister couldn't do. Nobody dragging my name through the gutter. Play with dog you get fleas for friend. I will have none of it. My name ain't Velasquez for nothing. Black as you see me I demand respect. I didn't get my name with no ring but with breeding. So exactly what you mean, Mr. Dr. Paul?

Dr. Paul: 'In Man we Burst' ain't sound so bad after all.

Spring: (*Enters*) Tantie, half pack a Anchor Special.

Tants: No trust.

Spring: Ay, ay since when?

Tants: Since now. You can't read? Well, hang up the sign, nuh. You playing signpost?

Spring: That ain't fair. You must give your regulars notice.

Tants: Spring, why you don't .... ask the government for notice?

Dr. Paul: Buy a papers and see. Look, flour, milk...

Spring: Alright! (*Taking out money*) Half pack.

Tants: Fifty cents.

Spring: Half of a pack.

Tants: You deaf?

Spring: It gone up?

Tants: 'PNM shake your balisier'.

Spring: Lawd! Gimme two stick instead.

Sparrow: *(At Club)* (NO DOCTOR NO)
Listen, listen carefully
I is a man does never be sorry
But I went and vote for some Councilmen
They have me now in the pen
After promising so much tender care
They forget me as they walk outa Woodford Square

Chorus:
They raise up on the taxi fare
No Doctor, no
And why the blasted milk so dear?
No doctor, no.
I want them to remember
We support them in September
They better come good
Because I have a big piece of mango wood.

Plenty, plenty people sorry
Sorry they throw down Big Belly
But not me, I sticking me pressure
When I can't buy milk I use sugar and water
Support local industry they done declare
They mean Vat 19 Rum and Carib beer
The way how they forcing we to drink Vat
It look like if they want to kill we in smart.

I only hope they understand
I am only a calypsonian
What I say may be very small
But I know that poor people ain't please at all

We are looking for a betterment
That is why we form a new government
But they raise on the food before we could talk
And they raise taxi fare so we bound to walk.

Sparrow: Ladies and gentlemen, we now have the ever
popular Lord Melody, Calypso King of 1954, to tell
us why you got to be careful in town these days. I
see Mr. Johhny Wright and his lovely lady in the
audience. You enjoying the show? From the horse's
mouth, ladies and gentlemen, the Lord Melody.

Melody: (PEDDLARS)
Beware of the peddlars in town }
A police nearly carry me down } Repeat
At the corner of George and Marine Square
A young man approach me there
When I think he was begging for charity
This is what the young man expose to me

He expose old boots, old shoes, an old pitch oil lamp
A suit from an old concentration camp
Needles, timbles, scissors and thread
A photograph of Sir Galba's head
Ashtrays, cigars, old picture frames
Walking sticks and an old switch blade
When he asked me what I was buying today
I tell him 'Mister, ah fraid'.

He had white wash, white lime, all kind of rag
A piece of a German flag
Pillow case, nighties, modess and socks
Rimless glasses, an old match box
Jingles, earrings, necklace and beads
Up came Constable Reid

He say 'Young man you got a lot of nice things there
That I really need.

But, where you get this Where you get that
Where did you get the Superintendent hat
This nightie look like my neighbour own
Where did you get that tenor saxophone
Let we go down, like you own the whole of town
This time me hand on me mouth
When I read the Evening News next evening
Was an old thief come down from South.

Wright: (*On stage, sporting Jean. Other calypsonians come forward.*)
Congrats, man, congrats. I booking you boys one
time for next Dimanche Gras, the biggest show of
Carnival. Sparrow as King, you in already. Sing 'No
Doctor'. I want the world to hear that song. Is not
only poor people what suffering from this damn
Communist Government.

Jean: Darling, shh.

Wright: Shh, what? This is still Trinidad. Free speech ain't mark
'For Blacks Only', right fellas? I depending on all you,
right? Let we go and take a drink. Bring the whole
damn side. Sparrow, sing a next verse in that song.

Sparrow: I don't sing for drink or for free. Mr. Wright, what is
the Calypso King prize for the next Dimanche Gras?

Wright: How you mean? What you get last year?

Sparrow: Twenty-five dollars and a silver cup.

Wright: That gone sky high man, like the cost of living.
This year the King getting a trip up the islands, a big

Murphy radio plus, three hundred and fifty dollars in cash and your cup. You could ask for more?

Sparrow: Plenty. The Queen, what in store for she?

Wright: Just what she was getting before, nothing more.

Christo: Nothing less neither.

Wright: What we have here? A showdown? Let we settle this over a drink.

Sparrow: We looking thirsty? Let we settle it right here. Time calypsonians stop living hand to mouth.

Wright: You see what this country come to? I come to celebrate and end up in the middle of an industrial dispute. So what more all you want? You get $25 last year. This year you getting $350 and about another thousand in opportunities. You still not satisfied?

Sparrow: Let the Queen rest with the Simmonds bed. We want more cash and the car.

Wright: Impossible. You fellas know anything about the running of this show? Is the businessmen who donate the prizes. You want to tell people how they must spend their money? Williams gone to all your head?

Jean: Darling, maybe...

Wright: Maybe what? Keep out of this.

Sparrow: Is over five thousand seats in that Grandstand and everybody paying.

Wright: And every cent goes to the Guardian Neediest Cases.
             You all want to rob the poor?

Sparrow: We is the poor!

Christo: And all we getting from your Committee is a raise in
             poverty.

Melody: Mr. Wright, watch me in my face and tell me if you
             find your offer is a fair deal.

Sparrow: Melo, that is a tall order. Anyhow, I make up my
             mind. Till all you could do better, much better,
             no Sparrow

             (CARNIVAL BOYCOTT) *(singers line up on Sparrow's side).*
             I will play me mas as usual   }
             Because I love Carnival   } repeat
             But no competition for me
             In San Fernando or the City
             They could preach Peter and Paul
             I wouldn't even go in the Savannah to see football

             Chorus:
             I intend to keep me costume on the shelf
             Let them keep the prize in Savannah for they
             own self
             And let the Queen run the show
             Without steelband or calypso
             Who want to go could go up they
             But me ain't going no way

             What really cause the upset
             Is the car the Queen does get
             She does nothing for Carnival

> She only pretty and that is all
> But men like me and you
> Saving money whole year to play Juju
> All we get is three case of beer
> And a talk-up as Band of the Year.

Jean: (*Applauds spontaneously.*)

Sparrow: And we putting on we own show. Time calypsonian
               make some money. On the Sunday night self this
               king will hold court! What you think we in this
               business for? Applause? (*Exits with retinue*)

Jean: King.

Wright: Who just now will be wondering where his kingdom
               gone. Ignorance in season. Come. (*She follows him off*)

Scene V

Williams: (*A meeting in the Square*) (THE BASE)
               Long long ago we didn't even know
               Not even a tip
               Nobody said Chaguaramas was exchanged
               For a few old battle ship
               So when we ask the Yankee to move
               Nobody really cares
               They refuse to go they say the Base is theirs
               Until 99 years.

               Chorus:
               So we ask the Chief Minister
               He say no, it isn't even register

It's not sealed nor stamp
Somebody is a big, big scamp
If they go remain
Let them take the Caroni swamp.

Great Britain, the Mother Country
That's the one to blame
It seems to me no matter what we do
They ain't feeling shame
They took the ships away from the Yanks
And promised them this place
But neglected to see the papers were signed
For the Chaguaramas Base.

Sparrow: *(Enters toward end of song.)*

Goldteeth: *(In crowd, briefcase, suit, hat, eight rings and a mouthful of gold, he smiles a lot. Whistles Sparrow over.)*

Sparrow: Goldteeth? That is you? You looking as good as your name.

Goldteeth: Your partner trying.

Sparrow: Try again. You ain't looking like no steelband captain. You looking more like the King of Calypso than me.

Goldteeth: I into a little business.

Sparrow: Whappen? What you selling? Insurance?

Goldteeth: Kinda. I hear you clash with Mr. Big?

Sparrow: If you mean that crook Johnny Wright and he Wrongside Committee, you damn right. If they ain't pay, I ain't singing and no Sparrow, no show. Simple as that.

Goldteeth: It ain't so simple. Word out on the streets that you getting too big for your boots. You have to look out, you mashing corns.

Sparrow: And I will stamp on them too. Me ain't fraid nobody, Gold. Let them come. I will beat them going and coming. Ten to one.

Goldteeth: Same ol Birdie, eh?

Sparrow: You tell them for me, me ain't change. I know the inside of a prison. So when they coming they better come good.

Goldteeth: Times change, though. Who street fighting these days? All over town is the big bang.

Sparrow: You think we in some Western? This is Trinidad.

Goldteeth: Look me card. You will need me.

(GUNSLINGERS) *(With A Chorus Of Badjohns)*
I selling guns nowadays   }
That's what really pays   } repeat
Nearly every young man is a gunslinger
With he razor and he steel knuckle on he finger
Don't mind they dress in suit and bow tie
All of them looking for guns to buy.

Chorus: We young and strong
We ain't fraid a soul in town
Who think they bad

To meet them we more than glad
I have me gun
And partner I ain't making fun
If you smart clear the way
Or if you think you bad make you play

If you don't believe me
Wait and you will see
They coming down by the crates
From quite in the States
I have me contact where they come from
I have me contact in the Custom
I have more contact than I can tell
Now I want to contact a place to sell

Chorus

Save your cash, save your cash
I selling razor, I selling cutlash
Sledgehammer, hatchet, even saw
Any kinda weapon that good for war
I done get me licence ever since
Now I only waiting for violence
Come to me and buy, don't be afraid
I selling from canon to razor blade.

Chorus

If you catch gun fever
Your two hand does start to shiver
This time you ready to attack
Like Audie Murphy in 'To Hell and Back'
If you see a man ain't fraid to get kill
Is to give him a one-way ticket to Boot Hill
Just get a couple of your friends
Swear him way, you did it in self-defence.

Tants: *(At the door of shop with chorus of women)*
(RUN THE GUNSLINGERS)
When talking 'bout mad it is I who mad
With these criminals that we have in La Trinidad
You can have a penny, you can have a pound
Bet you life them scamps going to knock you down
And when they do these things they goes around
Calling themselves famous men in town.

Chorus: When the police hold them
And they arrest them
Do not fine them
Don't imprison them
Send them in the Square
Let everybody be there
Beat them with the cat
And all who see bound to done with that.

Dr. Paul: I suppose that is the Government fault too?

Tants: Who else have them on the streets instead of
working somewhere or down Carerra?

Spring: And who send the Yankee home and have me back
on the streets? My trade getting hazardous. We
want protection! Eh Jean, eh Elaine?

Dr. Paul: You ain't want the Doctor heself as a escort?

Spring: Why not?

Dr. Paul: Oh lorse!

(DON'T BLAME THE PNM)
PNM in trouble
With some Trinidad people

The way they influence everybody
Some think everyday was free whisky
And I have to declare
Some think they will be living right in the air

Chorus:
Now Anabel stocking want patching
She want the Doctor help she with that
Johnson trousers falling
He want the Doctor help him with that
Some want a Zephyr motor car
Others want piece of land
Now Dorothy lost she man
She want to complain to Dr. Williams.

Because they put the party in power
They harrassing the poor Minister
Some so miserable
Like they want him perform miracle
The Indians who was the opposition
This is what they want from the young man
Carnival must be Ramleela
And turn all the schools to Maha Sabha

Scene VI

Sparrow: *(At club)* Tonight, is a special night, ladies and
gentlemen. This is the calypso show for the
calypsonians and you here to support us. Not no
high colour Carnival Queen. You the audience is
judge and jury. Look good at the man who say he
challenging Sparrow. You think I must take him in
serious?

(REPLY TO MELODY)
What is wrong with Lord Melody
And his reply to me
Its just a reply he jump and relate
I think the fella testing me faith
Because I sang about Dear Sparrow and the baby
He singing about Dear Lord Melody

Chorus:
But anything I do you follow   ing me
Behave your ugly self Melody
Do what you want but don't get me sore
Provocation is against the law
I married you went and you married too
But your wife ain't have eyes of blue
We have a lil chile you have one too
Anything I do this monkey does do.

You're a very good calypso singer
That we all know and will remember
But your face like a crocodile
And you looking so fierce and wild
I know you well and it ain't no lie
Your mouth always wide open catching fly
Try some deodorant it wouldn't hurt
Melody you smelling like a ramgoat

Melody: My looks, the man envy my looks. Between me and
he who better looking? You hear what the ladies say?

(SPARROW UGLY TOO.)
The men shout bring Sparrow!
The women shout out, no!
Mr. Bogowa going England
So they wanted two calypsonians

Farewell party to talk about
When a woman jump up and shout.

Chorus:
Sparrow could sing, but he is ugly too
Christo is nice, but his songs are few
When Melody sing, you could feel to your heel
Sparrow walk like a girl and his hair always press and
curl

The men flock Birdie
The women was around me
When I look back, poor Sparrow
Face like a green mango
Drink a Balisier, drink one again
This time Melody drinking champagne
All the women were meant for me
So I sent the waitress by he.

Sparrow: (MADAM DRACULA)
You went to St. Thomas, Melody
You pick up a bride
You went in the chapel
She was by your side
After you done married
You feeling O.K.
Tell your wife to listen
Carefully to what people say

Chorus:
When they see your madam walking
Middle of the street
People does stand up and watch down
At she crooked feet
People say she husband nose so spectacular
So everybody does call she, Madam Dracula

You went to St. Thomas
You carry Christo
Christo say your wedding
Was a pappyshow
With so much ol nigger
And so much of bum
All you had to eat was roti
And all you had to drink was rum.

Chorus

Then you bring the Yankee woman
Back to Trinidad
But none of your friends don't like her
She too old and hard
People say she husband nose perpendicular
And everybody does call she Madam Dracula.

Melody: (BELMONT JACKASS)
Man you married a tramp and you cable me to come
On the day of the wedding she loaded with rum
And the ring you presented was made outa brass
That is how I know your lousy wedding couldn't last.

Chorus:
Sparrow, when you wife walking
People say she shaking
She should wear a corset
For the goods she carrying
She should wear a harness
She face like a mas
That is why me boys does call she
Belmont Jackass!

Well the clothes that she wear on her gracious
wedding night

It was ramfle like hell and full of rat bite
With a short little dress all the men could see
And she drinking rum and water and watching at me.

(Switchblade gang on periphery of dance floor.
Music stops)

Gang: We looking for the best calypsonian in the world.

Sparrow: Melody!

Melody: Sparrow! *(Indicating each other, dancers clear floor)*

Both: Ask them! *(Indicating audience)*

Melody: Sparrow, I bow out. You really win. You is the best.
I gone. *(Exits)*

Sparrow: Well, everybody know I is the best. Where all you
from? The moon?

Gang: Nah, Royal Jail. Hangman Cemetery, Boot Hill
Remember there?

Sparrow: *(Looks around)* Look, what all you want? Money?

Gang: (GRENADIANS)
Chorus:
If you see how they holding the scamps and them
Friends you bound to bawl
Some of them could read and spell
But they can't pronounce at all
The policemen telling them say 'Hog, you stupid man'
And as you say 'Hag', licks in the police van.

Sparrow: All you can't do this! Is me, Mighty Sparrow!

Gang: Well, your cock done crow!
        Buss up he mouth!
        Lick out all he teeth!
        Spoil he sex life!
        Cramp he style!
        Cut off he competition!

Sparrow: *(Makes a dash for it. They pelt after him. A single shot is heard. Quiet. Returns, to a smoking tempo:)*

        (TEN TO ONE IS MURDER)
        Well they playing bad
        They have me feeling sad
        Well they playing beast
        Why they run for police

        Ten criminals attack me outside of Miramar
        (Ten to one is murder)
        About ten in the night on the fifth of October
        Way down Henry Street, by HGM Walker
        Well the leader of the gang was a hot like a pepper
        And every man in the gang had a white handle razor
        They say ah push they gal from Grenada
        Well, ah back back until ah nearly fall in the gutter
        You could imagine my position not a police in the area.

        Well ah start to sweat
        Man ah soaking wet
        Mama, so much threat
        That's a night ah never forget

        Ten ah them against me, with fifty spectators
        And the way they coming up like they want to devour
        But in the heat of the excitement is then ah remember
        In me next pants pocket I forget me wedger

Ah don't know what to do but I just can't surrender
Well they go cut me down just as small as Pretender
You could imagine how Ì they planning to dig out me liver.
But as the crowd start to gather ah started to shiver

In the still of the night
Ah was really in a fright
Me alone against ten
Ten vicious men

Ah remember ah had a chicken at Miramar
Well, ah said to meself, 'that was me last supper'
But ah get away and ah run, till ah reach
 Johnson corner,
They take off in me skin with big stick and boulder
The fella in front was a very good pelter
Bottle and stone falling but no place to shelter
Ah hear 'potow pow' and the crowd start to scatter!

(All Exit)

Act 2

Scene I

A pavement, the women collapse in laughter.

Marabunta: Ha, ha hai! *(Scandalously)* Take that in your backside!

Spring: Once more, once more, it sweet too bad.

Elaine: I go start this time. *They render a morose, mocking version of*

(ROBBERY WITH V)
They want a new King
They will do anything
Well they don't like the way how I sticking out
for money
If I don't get paid I ain't singing for nobody
They decide to clip me wing
And put a obstacle there as king.

Chorus:
A man with no originality
No stage personality
They trying to make me look small
All he have is a deep croon
But he won't change the tune at all
This song that song same melody, no variety
If you don't believe me you can ask anybody
If it ain't robbery with V

Marabunta: They say I'm not a sport
Call me names of every sort
But I want them to know
My whole life is calypso
I take it seriously
I don't care who say I silly
It's a job to me
No one should disagree
All I am begging them to do
Is to give credit where credit is due.

Elaine: Is time somebody else get a chance. You want to
reign you one forever?

Spring: Like he think he is the Doctor?

Marabunta: Nah. Jean Marabunta. *(They explode in laughter.)*

Chorus

He ain't have no originality

Dr. Paul: (*Hawking newspapers*) Sparrow's records seized! Read
all about it! Anti-Vice Squad say enough is enough!
Papers, lady?

Tants: (*In shop, reading*) 'Queen's Canary, Family-Size Coke,
Eye on the Middle Finger! (*Closing paper*) They
damn right. Sparrow too common.

Dr. Paul: Read all about it!

Spring: (*Entering*) The vice in their own head. Trinidad
people too damn hypocrite, eh Tants?

Tants: No damning in here this early morning. You say
your prayers?   And since when you and sun is
friend?

Spring: I get the shock of my life last night. I spot Lulu on
Marine Square selling alu and barra from basket. She
ain't here no more?

Tants: Lulu is a big entrepreneur, my chile. Always reaching
late because she had she own business going on the
side in San Juan. Soon as I find out I send she
packing.

Spring: Is so they does come, sweet sweet like they can't
mash ants and soon as they get the chance they dig
out your eye and leave you hanging high and dry like
something bat suck.

Tants: Not this Tantie. Nobody, man or woman
advantaging me.

Spring: I remember the time you put Kitchener in he place.

Tants: You mean out of this place. That worthless calypsonian.

Spring: (*Begins song, Tantie joins*)
(DON'T COME BACK AGAIN.)

Chorus:
Don't come back again, nigger man
Don't come back again
After you walk about and badtalk me name
You want to come back again

Tants: When I met you first, niggerman
You didn't have a pants
I labour as hard as I can
To give you a chance
All me privacy and inside secret
You tell the world of it
I rather live with a Carriacou
Than to take back a man like you.

I don't want no more niggerman
To come in me life
I don't think they quite understand
How to treat a wife
You could give them shelter and give them food
They got no gratitude
I promise not to be seen again
With another in Port of Spain.

Dr. Paul: Sales done for the morning. That pavement could do with a lil washdown. Tants, pass me the bucket.

Spring: Well, headlines 'City Intellectual Wash Down Pavement'

Dr. Paul: Just helping out now the lady alone, O.K.?

Spring: That self I come to see you about, Tants. Now Lulu gone you will need a waitress. I have experience, you know.

Tants: I have no luck with people, Spring. The only one I could depend on is myself and what strength God give me. Besides I could do without the extra expense. I saving every penny since Mr. Wright promise me first option on this place if he selling.

Dr. Paul: Independence frightening away plenty white people in true.

Tants: (*Turning papers*) The black ones better stay put. Look, four Blacks lynched in Alabama. (*Others share the papers*)

Spring: That United States stink with racism. A black Yankee marine heself tell me: They puts on powder, lipstick, rouge over their racism and calls it 'democracy'.

Dr. Paul: Soon, the sores will start bussing out all over their face. This is 1962!

Tants: Though the way some negroes up there behave they don't qualify for democracy. Can't read and wouldn't look to better they self.

Dr. Paul: That ain't the point. Democracy ain't democracy if is not for everybody. How long black people must suffer?

(MOCK DEMOCRACY)
Alabama, Alabama
I so glad I was born here
I have nothing against the United States
So listen carefully while I elucidate
Though Congress pass the Civil Rights Bill
Alabama subjugating my people still.

Chorus:
They profess to believe in a democracy
Yet refuse to recognise racial equality
Some people got together, form themselves a clan
Defied the laws of Congress to oppress
the coloured man
So looking back it makes me so glad
To belong to Tobago and Trinidad

In Alabama they show no mercy
For people like you and me
And in churches during High Mass
Suddenly you hear a big blast
Men, women and little children too
Running helter-skelter don't know what to do
When the orbituary next day is read
Fifteen big people injured, four children dead.

Well for instance, let's take Florida
And take a peep at what's going on there
And even some parts of Britain
They don't treat you like a human
They persecute and lynch you in Jacksonville
Torture you and frame you up in Nottinghill
Exercising inhumanity
And still they claim to believe in democracy.

Spring: All the same, if the Yankee send for me in the
morning I gone, yes. Any blasted place. So

much democracy down here I democratically catching hell. (*Exits singing*)

(B.W.I.A. SONG)
When I leaving Trinidad
For New York I will be feeling glad
With a Viscount plane relaxing my brain
Goodbye to Port of Spain.

Scene II

Sparrow: (*Cloaked, checks an address, presses buzzer. Is greeted by Melo*)

Melody: Boy, it good to see you. Barry giving you a try out tonight, before he sign you up. How long you here for?

Sparrow: A while. Them people back home too viperous! You hear how they thief my crown? Since is so they want it, I giving them a rest. I say let me see how green Uncle Sam back really is. What is the low-down?

Melody: Well, the man up here is Delamonte. He is the King of Calypso - which, by the way, is anything you sing with a straw hat, pretty shirt and plenty teeth in between. And you know the Yankees, stubborn in their ignorance. If they know 'Yellow Bird' as calypso, sing what you want, they ain't satisfied till they hear you tweeting. I never see a people ignorant so!

Sparrow: How this Delamonte does pay?

Melody: Chirrup-chirrup. The man have all my song and them and still owing me, but right now I can't do better.

Sparrow: Why you don't try somewhere else, man, Melo?
America is a big place, only the cold.

Melody: Lawd, and let them kill me? They does kill nigger
people here on the streets like dog, boy. Worse yet if
one of them women see you and like you? That is
death self! And you know Melo luck with the ladies
already? Not me!

Sparrow: Is so? I know down South was bad, but..........

Melody: South is the worst, but is all over, I tell you. Remember when I leave Trinidad I was heading for Miami?

(DISCRIMINATION)
Nobody asked me   }
How I spend my time in Miami } repeat
You know the food is nice, the drink is nice
Miami is paradise
But the colour question there
Brother I rather here

Chorus:
You know you can't sit down there
You can't stand up there
You can't go in there
Nigger, read and write
Drive in the back
Your face is too black
Walk in the dark
Nigger read and write

Sparrow: Well, I ain't the man to take that just so and swallow
it. It have two island in the West Indies I could go
back to any day. What about Canada? I hear there
ain't bad.

Melody: Ain't bad for the penguins. If you think here cold, put foot in Canada.

Sparrow: Remember what you tell me that first time we meet in Tantie Shop?

Melody: You remember?

Sparrow: Calypso is you the singer, your story.

Melody: Look, Delamonte on now. He bringing you on after he sing so the audience wouldn't even want to hear you.

Sparrow: My mind make up. I here to make some good money and I ain't leaving till I get it. Colour-line, Delamonte, cold combine ain't turning me back. I is Sparrow and calypso is my story!

Delamonte: (SHAME AND SCANDAL)
In Jamaica there was a family
With much confusion as you will see
There was a mama and a papa and a boy
who had grown
Who wanted to marry and have a wife of his own
So he went to his papa, the papa said 'No,
That girl is your sister but your mama don't know.'

Chorus:
Woe, woe woe, woe is me   }
Shame and scandal in the family. } repeat

So he continued searching the rest of his life
Because he really needed a wife
He met a wonderful girl with lovely figure
But afraid to consult his dear father
He met a lovely darkie which was twice as nice

He flew to the papa to get his advice
When the papa see the girl he shout 'Oh no,
That girl is you sister but your mama don't know.'

So he went to the mama, the mama shook she head
When she found out what her husband had said
So she paused for a moment undecidedly
This time the boy waiting patiently
Then the mama she laughed and said 'Go, man, go,
Your daddy ain't your daddy but your daddy don't
know'

We close the first half of our show with a special
guest, a native calypso singer from the West Indies,
where it all started way back in the dark ol' days, a lot
like the Blues. Fresh from the coconut isles of the
sunny West Indies, welcome to New York, the Mighty
Sparrow!

Sparrow: (NO MORE ROCK AND ROLL)
I say calypso sweeping the place}
Like if she from outa space   } repeat
I can remember rock and roll
Had the whole place under control
Since calypso leave Trinidad
Rock and roll suffering bad

Chorus:
No more rocking, no more rolling, no more jumping
up like a fool
Whether you lazy, or you crazy you just got to
take it cool
This is calypso and every one know it is strictly
rhythm and rhyme
Whether young or old, jump in the line and
shake your body in time.

Plenty people trying their best
But they making a mess
Just for the money they'll put on a show
And tell you it's calypso
But you must come to Trinidad
See how the people jumping mad
For as soon as we hear the true melody
The jumping spirit comes naturally.

Mr. Delamonte says calypso is a little like the Blues
and he's right. Now more than ever Americans got
reason to sing the Blues, and we too in the
West Indies. Tell me, you people look very smart,
what's one from ten? Well where I come from one
from ten leaves nought.

(FEDERATION)
People want to know why Jamaica run
From the Federation
Jamaica have a right to speak she mind
That is my opinion
And if you believe in democracy
You'll agree with me

Chorus:
But if they know they didn't want federation
And they know they didn't want to unite as one
Tell the Doctor you not in favour, don't behave like a
blasted traitor
How the devil you could say you ain't federating
no more?

When they didn't get the capital site
That nearly cause big fight
When Sir Grantley Adams took up his post
That even make things worse (they bawling)

We ain't want no Bajan Premier
Trinidad can't be capital for here
So the grumbling went on and on
To a big Referendum

Federation boil down to simply this
It's dog eat dog survival of the fittest
Everybody fighting for Independence
Singularly, Trinidad for instance
We go get it too so don't bother
But I find we should all be together
Not separated as we are
Because of Jamaica.

Scene III

*All outside shop preparing banner and costumes for band
called 'Independence'. (Pan in a slow chip)*

Spring: Aye! Like they starting up! *(goes off)*

Goldteeth: *(Dancing the flag)* So push them blues down your back
                pocket and unbutton your bacchanal, wind your
                worries round your waist, woman roll them bass
                drums God give you and is down the road,Bobolups!

Tants: Dr. Paul, you able?

Dr. Paul: Watch me.

Tants: Just keep your eye on the property, please.

Dr. Paul: Lord, that pan sounding sweet!

Spring: (*Leaving band*) Tantie! Kitch! Kitch in town!

Tants: Which Kitch that?

Spring: Lord Kitchener, nuh! You playing you don't know? The same Kitchener who you run from you door mouth! Come and tell me if I lie.

Tants: Who tell you I want to see any watless calypsonian? Where him?

Spring: With the hat.

Tants: You sure?

Spring: I talk to the man.

Tants: Not that I really interested, but I have to see that scamp with my own two eye. Dr. Paul, mind the shop a minute for me please. (*Exits to street*)

Dr. Paul: Like I playing mamapoule? Dr. Paul time to declare your hand. (*Exits*)

Wright: (*Costumed, on street*) Jean! Jean! Where that bitch gone? Anyway is Carnival, so what the hell! You see mas? (*Displays*) You see dance? 'The Glories of Independence'! 'West Indian Federation' could ever touch this? Licks like fire! But where this woman? She must be feel because the band name 'Independence' I must dance by myself? Wait, nuh, that is my section? (*Squints ahead*) Lockjoint Scandal' Cheap mas. 'Best Village Vanguard'. Foot soldiers, man, low class. Which one is this? 'Federation is Botheration'. Ah hah, that look like mine . . . . yes, yes, 'Lords of the Realm of Bobol' mas fada! That blasted woman better find me and fast! (*Exits dancing*).

Kitch: (*Jumping with Tantie*) (THE ROAD)

Chorus:
The road make to walk on Carnival day
Constable I don't want to talk but I have to say
Any steelbandman
Only venture to break this band
Is a long funeral
From the Royal Hospital

Dr. Paul: (*In Pierrot Grenade gown and mask blocks their way*)
Nobody pass unless you pay
With the one word I want to say.

Tants: I know your voice, Mr. Mas. If it ain't Dr. Paul I calling police right away for your...

Dr. Paul: Don't call no massa, why you heart so hard? I is just a mamapoule, a foolosopher with something he want to tell you bad, bad.

Tants: Who tell you I want to hear anything bad this Carnival day? (*To Kitch*) You remember Dr. Paul? Well, is the fool he come out to play.

Kitch: Pierrot Grenade. You know how long I ain't see this mas?

Dr. Paul: Long, long time longer than a rope that stretch from here to Grenada, I want to say...don't play you don't know. Is small but the best word in the world. You don't know it, sah?

Kitch: Mas

Dr. Paul: Close but not class enough. This word, you see, any Carnival it does outlast, fuss it long, long, long after the singer gone it still around. How much years since Cleopatra taste a serpent kiss? Let the police come. How long I at your door with my two hand tie up at the wrist?

Tants: This man gone mad?

Dr. Paul: Door is do, wris' is ris

Kitch: Or in love

Dr. Paul: Ai ya yai!

(LOVE AND MISS DOVE)
Chorus:
I told her love is a ocean full of motion
Well attached to the police station
It swells like a whale it crawls like a snail
And it leads both lovers inside the jail.

Tants: *(allows Dr. Paul to take her away.)*

Kitch: (MAMA DIS IS MAS)
Mama dis is mas
I say it's mas of class
And this I can assure
It's what you hoping for
We ain't have no fight or fuss
Visitors can join with us
And jump up in the bacchanal
And enjoy the Carnival

Chorus:
Mama the bands will be passing down
Frederick Street

With a ping pong beat
In the burning heat
And they march merrily to the Savannah
No one aggressive
Carnival is strictly conservative

When you miss Kitchie
Don't bother look for me
Because I in the band
Hugging some man woman
If he get to know
I still ain't letting go
He have to wait until I play
He go get she Ash Wednesday.

(All exit)

Marabunta, Spring bounce up

Marabunta: You ain't see who back in town, girl?

Spring: Kitch. That is stale news. I see him first.

Marabunta: Which Kitch? Look good. Watch how the white woman hold on to him.

Spring: O God, the ol' hog.

Marabunta: That dutty dog. *(Together)* Sparrow! We boy!

Sparrow: Me and all you? I gone for higher!

Spring: Haul you tail! Kitch reach back!

Sparrow: That ol' timer could only sing road march. When it come to social commentary, Sparrow rule this roost!

And I go comment on all you tail!
(*Exits with Jean*)

Scene IV

Kitch: (*Spot*) (BAD IMPRESSION)
The old people say
What ain't happen in years
Happen in a day   } repeat
Say what you like you can't doubt them
Just look at the big murder problem
Never happen before
Trinidad changing into an outlaw.

Chorus:
It's a bad impression
On a new born nation
To be having murders almost everyday

When you read the blackboard
And you check the records
On an average we worse than the USA
The Government must intervene it's imperative
For we are even scared to walk on the streets we live
The way things are going
It is so terrifying
I don't believe its going to cease,
The fashion is murder, murder, police , Police!

Last February
A visit to my homeland terrified me
Every blessed day
Murder is the headline the papers say

The last incident I remember
They shoot a well know Chinee fella
What an atrocity
Police and all in the murder spree

It was told to me
Criminals today are at liberty
Promptly without fail
They obtain high class treatment in the jail
Well if this is really on the level
How on earth will they set an example
Such action is only mad
It's encouraging the crime wave in Trinidad.

Scene V

Tants: (*Enters shop, slowly. Sits heavily*) I went to the Bank. Yes, that same bank they call Barclays. The lil scrapings I get from the teashop, is there it save, as you know. I stand in the line. It wasn't short. My varicose giving me hell, but I tell myself, I say, 'Doris, is you and you alone. If you can't take it, then who is to take it for you?' Show the cashier my book and tell she, not loud, I want to borrow some money.

Dr. Paul: The cashier, what she look like?

Tants: Light, cashier-colour type. Up and down she watch me with something Grannie talk about in she eyes. 'Borrow money? Not here. The Loans Section is over there.' Just so, loud, so the rest of the line could hear. 'Next'. In the Loans Section, the

Secretary finish typing a page before she answer my
'Good morning.' A Chinese lady who I does see in
Church every Godbless Sunday. I show she my
book, tell she.....she say the Manager too busy, but
she need information. Sit. She ask where I born?
My father, if he living or dead and my mother too.
Where they was from? If I married or common law,
widowed or divorced? My husband, when last I see
or hear from he? How much children I have, their
ages and who else dependent on me? How much the
shop does bring in and how I spend it? How much
in rent? Food? Medicine? Other necessities? Who
I owe? Who owe me? Why I want the loan? If I
know anybody else with account at the bank or if
anybody of account know me? If I own car, land,
house with insurance against fire and hazard and if I
ever borrow money in that Bank before? (*Pause*) Yes,
Dr. Paul today I went to the bank.

Scene VI

Kitch: (*At Country Club*)
              TRINIDAD IS COOL AND QUIET
              All about is race riot
              Trinidad is cool and quiet
              I pinpoint America
              B.G. and Rhodesia
              The situation is really sad
              But they must take example from Trinidad.

              Chorus:
              Because the Doctor say and I think he's right
              Tolerance is our policy

We love it this way both the black and white
So we must live in unity.

Sparrow: (*Sparrow and Jean enter*)
This old man is trouble, yes. I sure now he ain't wash-up.

Jean: Everybody know Kitch was tops when he leave here.

Sparrow: Was. Right now he is only an opponent worthy of a king. (*Laughs*) How I looking?

Jean: Like a king. King Sparrow. My king.

Sparrow: The Country Club! Look where calypso and pan reach nuh,. You think Kitch or any calypsonian before me coulda tell white people how much they must pay him to sing at their Country Club? And talk the truth, doux, doux, you coulda see yourself walking in here with Kitch? Or Melo?

Jean: And why not?

Sparrow: Looks apart, people woulda call you a jamette.

Jean: They will still do it.

Sparrow: Tell them, that car you come here in, the Black Label we was sipping, my mansion and that king-size bed not no Simmonds bed all come from calypso money. No thiefing or bobol like some of them inside there. Every cent mint from my talent.

Jean: What I really hate is being boxed in. I'm born with a white skin so I'm a Carnival Queen and I must sleep with Johnny Wright. I'm with you so I'm a jammette. I don't give a damn. None of that mean anything to me.

Sparrow: Well, it mean a damn lot to me and no ghost from the past coming to inherit my kingdom.

Wright: (*Addresses audience*). And so on my Government's behalf I take this opportunity to welcome you and encourage your interest in this paradise of the Caribbean. Our relationship with the United States has always been one of mutual respect. We are friendly, virgin territory awaiting the thrust of U.S. investment. You will find our people malle. . .malleable (*Stumbles in reading*) fun-loving but hard-working, our economy receptive and the stablest Government anywhere in the region...Who the arse does write these speeches boy? Now for what we do best. You heard our wonderful steelband, the only musical instrument invented in this century. Now two of our leading calypsonians, kings in their own right Lord Kitchener and the Mighty Sparrow!

Sparrow: (*Stepping out*) This is a story I read in the papers not so long ago. A certain calypsonian had the nerve to attack the Mighty Sparrow. Sparrow, your days are numbered, he said, you're going down and I come back from England.

Kitch: (*Stepping out*) And I come back from England, I'm going to take your crown

Sparrow: Kitchie, boy, no more skylarking. Come out in the open. This time is the time and the place.

Kitch: You come to trouble trouble, young man? Take care I don't make you dingolay down the line.

Sparrow: Ol' talk! I is King Sparrow, as everybody know, the born regent of calypso! When I was just one the stars declare . . .

Kitch: Stay in Grenada, for Kitchie rule over here! I ain't interested in your biography, young man. I will play All Fours with your metaphors. Place your money.

Sparrow: Ten to one!

Kitch: And I double that ! Calypso for calypso let we see who have song to wine this action down!

Sparrow: Kitchie, your death warrant just sign. You ain't have much time left. So best you start.

Kitch: Fresh and hurry-come-up! This race ain't for the fast but for who could last. Take this lesson from the master! Brips! Music!

(NO MORE CALYPSONG)
Stop this stupid calypsong
Everybody say you wrong
Try your best and co-operate
Keep this culture up to date
Don't sing classic and ballad
Can't fool the folks of Trinidad
Trinidadians bound to know
What is really calypso.

Chorus:
No more calypsong
The public bawling for murder
They say to bring back the ol time mi minor
They beg me to come down from England
To teach the method to all calypsonian

Bring more bounce especially
Less bars in your melody
Don't stray all entirely
From the correct harmony
Change that voice in which you sang
Get that real calypso twang
And perhaps you'd like to know
Then you singing calypso

Chorus:
No more calypsong
The public bawling for murder
They say to bring back the ol time mi minor
You crucifying Trinidad
With your tango, carol, classics and ballad

Sparrow: (MR. KITCHENER)
Tell me what is wrong   }
With some of them old time calypsonian } repeat
It's a different era now
They come back here making row
They'll regret they beg me for war
I go beat them like a child 1964

Chorus:
Clear the road, lemme pass, Mr. Kitchener
You stepping outa your class
Kitchie boy, you gone too far
Ol timer you gone
I say your days done
Clear the road lemme pass, Mr. Kitchener.

Calypso is me
And I am calypso in this country
It is I does carry the load
Every year with a set of tunes on the road

Kitch ain't got a thing to lorse
He come like Mentone, once upon a time he was a
good horse
But now that he old
I am the Calypso King of the World

(*Kitchener exits. Jean and Goldteeth come forward to congratulate Sparrow*)

Wright: (*Confronting Goldteeth*) What you doing on this side man?

Goldteeth: How you mean? I come to talk to my pardner...Wright: But who is you?

Sparrow: Is alright, Mr Wright, he come to me.

Goldteeth: Goldteeth. (*Smiles*). Is my band out there playing.

Wright: Alright hell! He here to beat pan and out there in the yard is for pan. This is a special government function, man, Country Club, not the Savannah. I ain't want you fellas mingling with the guests.

Jean: Diplomacy was never your strength, Johnny Wright.

Wright: Look, I lil too busy to stroll down memory lane with you. You know the way.

Goldteeth: Well, to hell with you.

Wright: You better get out! You think you could play badjohn in here? Guard!

Sparrow: Mr Wright, that ain't called for, we could work this thing out.

Wright: It done work out. But where the arse this guard is?

Sparrow: I ain't like that, man.

Wright: Look, you ask for damn good money to come here tonight and we agree. So what you want to do? Go with your pally-wally here or do what you say your job is and sing?

Sparrow: All I saying is that it ain't necessary to throw the man out so. That ain't the way, man.

Wright: Mr Francisco, make up your mind. I ain't paying you to advise on protocol.

Jean: Darling

Sparrow: Look, you keep outa this.

Wright: Not everything as easy as changing beds, eh Jean?

Jean: I won't stand for this. (*Walks off*)

Wright: Marabunta. We have a contract, Mr Francisco.

Sparrow: Gold, this is my living.

Goldteeth: (*Smiles*). And this is my life. I gone but the pan gone with me.

Wright: Ask yourself Mr Goldteeth, which part of Trinidad and Tobago you will find a next sponsor tomorrow.

Goldteeth: (*Pauses. Exits*)

Wright: (*Locks eyes with Sparrow for a beat*) Look Sparrow, I have no problem with you. In fact, let me introduce

you to my guests. We ain't have no colour bar in
Trinidad, right?

*Sound of pan music in background as Sparrow moves to the
podium.*

Sparrow: I ain't know what kind of bar you call it, but from
the end of the world I sing, it feel like the same
damn thing.

(OUTCAST)
Society in Trinidad for a steelbandman
Was just as hard or even harder than that
For any calypsonian
Don't care how you talented you must go outside
You get no appreciation here
Society had too much false pride

Chorus:
Calypsonians really catch hell for a long time
To associate yourself with them was a big crime
If your sister talk to a steelbandman
The family want to break she hand
Put she out, lick up every teeth in she mouth
Pass, you outcast.

The reason why I say false pride is simply this
They enjoy your song, enjoy your music and still
They so damn prejudice
They bracket you in a category so low and mean
Man they give the impression
That your character is unclean

Scene VII

Lulu: *(Changes sign from 'Tantie's Teashop' to 'Oriental Delites'. she is very busy)* I put it down to luck. I didn't even know the place was up for sale all that time. Since I on my own I hardly come to this side. But Second Spring see me and tell me like Tantie can't keep the place. I went back Carapo, you know and beg my uncles to help me out. Well the rest you could see.

Scene VIII

Woodford Square. A group of women in white gowns and headties. A tin plate and candle on the ground.

Marabunta: (BORN TO BE.)
I am really no prophet
But I am quite sure of this
Some people just were born to be kings
Others were born to be suffering
But like this thing start from Creation
And wouldn't stop til the world's to end.

Some people born to be happy
And to live in luxury
Others just were born to be
Poor and live in misery
When I born my mother said
My child, you will suffer till you dead
So you see the reason why
I suffering bad and I don't cry.

I now see the world is round
That's why things up-sided down

> Maybe if it was flat and square
> Everyone get an equal share
> Some people wouldn't like things that way
> Have everything and wouldn't give away
> But the higher they are the harder they fall
> They sure have to dead and leave it all.

(*She stares with the eyes of the blind*)

Sparrow: (*Stops. Approaches*). Jean Marabunta?

Marabunta: Ah, the King! Tonight is my lucky night. What you doing here among commoners? You come to leave something with your girl?

Sparrow: I really hear you in retirement. Or I should still make that a question?

Marabunta: Your girl still in town. I really hear they kick your arse out the Country Club the other day.

Sparrow: You hear wrong. Tell whoever spreading that ol' talk they lie.

Marabunta: That self I tell them. But you know nigger people how they mauvais langue. They say you playing white man.

Sparrow: Me? Look at my crosses. You ain't see my skin?

Marabunta: Same thing I say. Sparrow can't forget the ground he piss fall on, that mother him and waiting for him to come. And I ain't need no eyes to see the truth in that. But you know it hard to hear anything else when money talking.

Sparrow: I had my contract ready for that tail. It woulda be me, them and the law, (Pause). All the change we change, Jean, nothing ain't change.

Marabunta: So you come here?

Sparrow: This is where it started, in this Square.

Marabunta: Back to square one.

Sparrow: I was just wondering...

Marabunta: Where it went wrong? All you hear what the king asking, sisters?

Sparrow: *(Among Sisters)*. Wait, uh that ain't Tantie? And Jean? You too? You walk out on me to come here?

Marabunta: And Hog-Face Elaine, Big Eye Mable, Pickey-Head Eileen and Stinking-Mouth Doreen. All who calypso and life pitch out on the streets.

Jean: They accept me. My looks and colour didn't matter.

Marabunta: You see we colour blind. We does gather here on a evening, give we lil thanks and share a word or two with all who care to listen.

Sparrow: Keep up the good work. Look I leaving something on the plate. *(Drops coins)*

Marabunta: Still tight as a fleas's arse.

Sparrow: That's all I have.

Marabunta: Lies. But that's the world we build.

Sisters: (MASSA DAY MUST DONE)
We used to boast about our land
Saying we have racial integration
We told the world that our country
Is an example of love peace and racial harmony
But all that's now a fake
The Country Club issue make us wide awake
But that's a drop of water, my friend
In an ocean of discrimination.

Marabunta: You want to know how it went wrong? You see, it
was never right from the start. How a hardworking
woman like Tantie could end up on the streets
because the banks turn she down?

Sisters: The Country Club is joke there are many more
Banks give us loans based on our colour
To get certain lawyers to defend you in court
The colour of your skin and prestige is your passport
Massa in hotel
Drinking run and whiskey and he living well
And poor man catching he tail
And if he thief to live they throw him in jail

Sparrow: So what I must do about that that I ain't doin now? I
fighting since I born and not a damn thing change.

Marabunta: You see why I had to whore, sisters? You does have
to take black man in bits and parts. None of them
whole, none of them wholly able.

Sparrow: Madam, you have money to lorse in court?

Sisters: Let's face the facts brother look around
Some youths have jobs others have none
To get a job poor girls have to sin

While in most stores and banks you see one race and
same skin
Rich men getting way
With cockfight, churches gambling on harvest day
And police in your tail whole day
If you only play whapee and whe-whe.

Marabunta: All of them want to be king before they learn to be
man. So we telling you 'King Calypso' that whatever
else ain't change, we is a new story, a new song. Sing
that. (*They stand illumined like the queens they are*) Who
else must we ask? We here waiting on no King, no
massa. We here waiting like all whores, on a man.

Sisters: So please won't yu tell them massas
Massa day must done
We want no racialism in our country
No prejudice or colour bar must divide we
The land must belong to everybody
So tell the Portuguese Club to come off our island
To hell with Chang Sang and Chinese Association
This land only have room for us West Indians
We want no division
Massa day must done.

Sparrow: (*Seeing them*) Elaine Nightingale, Honey Doreen,
Sweet Voice Jean, how it is I never see or hear this
before? (*To Marabunta*) How come, Sister Jean?

Marabunta: We and all didn't know who we was. Now looking
inside we know. (BLACK IS BEAUTIFUL)
A many many years it took
For us go get that natural look (repeat)
Now suddenly out of the blue
This thing has struck like something new

                     Everybody young and old
                     Going afro and telling the world

Sisters: Black is beautiful
                    Look at the gloss
                    Black is beautiful, it's texture of us
                    Lift your head like we
                    You got to wear your colour with dignity
                    Black is beautiful, look at the shine
                    Black is beautiful, it's yours and it's mine
                    It's high time that we
                    Get rid of this old slave mentality.

Sparrow: Give thanks.

Marabunta: (*Pointing*) The earth.

Sparrow: (*Stoops and touches the earth*)

Elaine: Now you could start by saying you sorry for all them
                    jagabat name you call we.

Sparrow: Sorry? If wasn't for me how the hell this change
                    coulda happen? You should be down on your knees
                    thanking me. And let me talk my mind. With all the
                    sweet voice you think any of you could make a
                    decent back-up side in my calypso tent? (*General melee
                    as they rush to beat him*) Beg pardon, beg pardon, I only
                    joking. Ten to one is advantage.

Sisters: (TEN TO ONE)
                    Well you playing bad
                    We have you going mad
                    Yes you playing beast
                    But don't run for police

Sparrow: (Breaksing) These sisters attack me cause I bad talk
             them pardner.
             Ten to one is murder etc

             (All join chorus for the curtain)